For my wife, Elaine,

and our daughters, Isabella and Veronica,

whom we loved before they were born,

and to my father and mother,

Alfio and Josephine Cardillo

The 12 Rules of Attention

How to Avoid Screw-Ups, Free Up Headspace, Do More, and Be More at Work

Joseph Cardillo, PhD
author of
Can I Have Your Attention? and
Be Like Water

NICHOLAS BREALEY
PUBLISHING

BOSTON • LONDON

First published in the United States of America in 2020 by Nicholas Brealey Publishing

An Hachette company

24 23 22 21 20 1 2 3 4 5 6 7 8

Author photo on page 215 courtesy of Siobhan Connally Photography

Library of Congress Control Number: 2020933362

ISBN 9781529361995
U.S. eBook ISBN 9781529362022
U.K. eBook ISBN 9781529362015

Printed in the United States of America

Nicholas Brealey Publishing policy is to use papers that are natural, renewable, and recyclable products and made from wood grown in sustainable forests. The logging and manufacturing processes are expected to conform to the environmental regulations of the country of origin.

Disclaimer
The case examples in this book are drawn from media accounts or are composite examples based upon behaviors encountered in the author's own professional experiences. None of the individuals described was a client. The names and details have been changed to protect the privacy of the people involved.
    This publication does not claim medical advice. This book is not and should not be used as a substitute for the business advice of authorized employment consultants and/or human resource advisers. It is not intended as a substitute for the advice of such healthcare and/or business professionals.
    Before engaging in any business, physical, psychological, or spiritual training programs, you should always check with your own professional business and employment advisers as well as physicians and professional healthcare providers to be sure that they are right for you.

Nicholas Brealey Publishing
Carmelite House
50 Victoria Embankment
London EC4Y 0DZ
Tel: 020 7122 6000

Nicholas Brealey Publishing
Hachette Book Group
53 State Street
Boston, MA 02109, USA
Tel: (617) 523 3801

www.nbuspublishing.com

CONTENTS

INTRODUCTION

For more than a decade, businesses have zeroed in on the stunting effect of today's focus-starved brains. How could they not? The statistics are staggering. A recent PayScale survey, for example, based on responses from 63,924 managers, reported that 56 percent of college grads do not pay attention to detail at work.[1] Add to that the cost of error. Companies in the United States pay a whopping $650 billion per year for errors attributed to employee distraction.[2] That doesn't even cover the full extent of the inattention problem to organizations. As far as organizations are concerned, employees with high-quality attention skills have become a commodity. *The 12 Rules of Attention* is prescriptive and written specifically for entry-level to mid-management businesspeople. To this end, this book will help you train your attention to sharp, accurate, and high definition and keep it there. But I promise you, this attention story doesn't stop with just avoiding workplace flub-ups.

The other side of the attention picture is you—do you feel like you're crushing it? How productive, happy, and fulfilled do you feel each day at the workplace? You might ask what attention has to do with it. This is a legitimate question. The answer may help clear up and *fix* a wide range of ongoing personal workplace concerns—including and well beyond work error. Simply put, attention is connected to every single thing you think, feel, and do at work and elsewhere. It's almost impossible to imagine, but by the end of this book I hope that you not only understand how this is so but also are enjoying getting into your mind's attentional machine and regulating it to your highest advantage. Consider this fact: you are either regulating this mental faculty yourself or it is regulating you.

Perhaps at this point you are wondering, "Then why isn't everyone out learning all they can about training their attention?" Here's the thing: whether you walk around work all day feeling like a zombie or like you have the energy of a nuclear reactor, whether you glide through your day or have a day that feels straight out of Dante's *Inferno*, most of what goes on in your brain as you attend to things is happening under your radar—subconsciously. This is the dark, cavernous place where your brain's attentional network lives and sparks. When our workday is going great, most of us, no matter how smart we are, ignore all this incredible activity going on in our skull. IQ doesn't have much to do with it either. Furthermore, we seldom ask, "What could I have done to make things turn out better?" It's not until endeavors start really messing up that an alarm goes off in our head and we start wondering, "What's going on?" and "What was I thinking?" and "What can I do to get back on track?"

TRY THIS!

Take a moment and have some fun with this little activity. For each question below, rapidly say aloud the first thing that comes to mind. Keep going—*rapidly*—until you finish.

What color is a cotton ball?
What color is a piece of typing paper?
What color are marshmallows?
What color is a wedding dress?

What color is snow?
What do cows drink for breakfast?[3]

Eight out of 10 people answer *milk* to the last question and find themselves chuckling at their answer as soon as they say it. There are quite a few different versions of this game. The point, however, is the same: the riddle is designed to help you literally feel how your mind decides things when you are not attending to them. In the world of work, another example is when you say *yes* too soon to a coworker when you already know you are taking on too much work or when you suddenly divulge more information than you should. The fact is, such decisions are made for you without your input all day long. Most people aren't aware of just how much is determined this way. For example, your brain's attentional system can determine whether you feel depressed or spirited; how you experience others (and how they experience you); the depth, frequency, and accuracy of your insights (or whether you have any insights at all); as well as your frequency of workplace error, successes, and development. Cumulatively these determine your workplace happiness and ability to grow professionally. The question is, "Are you controlling them, or are they controlling you?" If I have learned anything in the last two decades of attention research, it's that we can at least gain control of important moments in living. Learning this skill and putting it into practice will make a big difference in your daily successes.

Evolution has gifted every healthy brain (which most of us enjoy) with the capacity to control what we pay attention to and the quality of our focus. This capacity is driven by our *executive attention*—the ability to select one detail over another even if we have to override the temptation of stronger urges. Think of it as your focus's CEO. This mechanism gives you a lot to say about the quality of your focus and how your workday goes.

Consider this: Gallup's recent annual report shows 55 percent of workers in the United States report feeling stressed on their job.[4] More than half of US workers are dissatisfied with their jobs.[5] Astonishingly 82 percent of us feel our strongest talents go wasted at the workplace—all attention-related problems.[6]

These issues often snowball into further problems, including these:

- Worker absenteeism, tardiness, and burnout
- Decreased productivity
- Workers' compensation claims
- Increased employment turnover
- Medical insurance costs from work-related stress

It's all related. When you experience your work as unhappy and stressful, it's hard to pay good attention to the tasks at hand. When you're not paying quality attention, it's easy to experience more displeasure and slip into a downward cycle. However, a little knowledge about how your attentional machinery works and how you can manage it will go a long way. *The 12 Rules of Attention* will show you both.

YOU DON'T HAVE TO THROW OUT YOUR DEVICES

The contemporary wail for more than a decade has been that workplace distractions and errors are largely technology's fault. But there is certainly more to the story. The challenge today is that all along the work chain, individuals are fading out mentally and emotionally. We've been giving the full weight of the blame for our distraction to technology far too long now. I prefer more of a reductionist approach for getting to the bottom of today's low-attentional wattage. From this perspective, I am cautious about stopping with technology as the sole culprit. I don't think we are going to change much if we do. Remember, it was just a generation ago that cable television programming suffered the same rap. Before that it was general television, radio, and telephones. In fact, every generation since Sophocles could make similar arguments about the attention-stealing aspects brought on by progress.

Just for fun, imagine back, through an evolutionary lens, an early human whose brain had about the same cognitive horsepower as ours. Picture that person trying to stay focused while, say, hunting a deer. Imagine the disrupting impact of just a few environmental obstacles, such as heat, cold, rain, insects, and other creatures sharing the environment. All of these elements would be capable of throwing emotional and cognitive interruption (and rumination) into attempted daily goals. There has always been an overload of detail. There has always been distraction. There has always been a need for selecting where we need to aim our attention.

Some scientists believe that our attentional decline is the result of idiocracy—actions that come from someone else's (or some previous generation's) ideas that were problematic to begin with. We all have some of these floating around in our head. One of the most common, for example, is the mantra "No pain, no gain." We use this everywhere, from business to athletics to education. Physiologically speaking (as well as athletically) this couldn't be further from the truth. In fact, if you work out and feel pain and just keep on rockin' anyway, then you are running the risk of traumatizing muscles and joints as well as causing greater injury. The list of idiocracies, of course, goes on. Problem is, they can keep you spinning your wheels in yesterday's dysfunctional thinking when you are trying to get ahead.

I don't have a beef with claims that technical devices have added to contemporary distraction. But they are far from the totality of the problem. I completely support, with fellow parents, the careful monitoring and restricted use of such devices in the hands of children, and I share in the full range of psycho-physical developmental concerns with regard to their use. Further, *The 12 Rules of Attention* does not argue with the disruptive capability of devices sounding off or flashing as we are busy with daily tasks or with the personal and institutional consequences of individuals who are preoccupied with checking out unnecessary email or making needless calls during the workday. However, these activities are symptomatic and not root causes. *We won't neglect them, but I'm after bigger fish.*

On the other hand, there is a surplus of research supporting that new advances in technology offer potential for even faster, more precise focus and learning skills. This upshot is equally very likely to be less talked about or explored. As with so many of life's tools, it's not the technology that's eating up brain power—it's how you use it.

In the coming chapters, you will look at a range of basic (more organic) causes for inattention. The book's 12-rule format shows you how to achieve and maintain sharp, crisp, and accurate attention, especially for important moments in your workday.

You will learn

- How to use your entire attentional system, beyond just focus (which is only one part)
- How to avoid fading out
- How and when to employ awareness, mindfulness, and attention, which are three separate things
- A process to relieve data overflow, internal distraction, and external distraction

- How to use your in-a-glance mental capacity to catch more desired detail
- How to regulate your brain's automatic, high-speed attention triggers and use them to your advantage
- And more...

Yes, I will mention how technology can consume workplace focus and what you can do to make yourself less vulnerable. But I promise you that the spotlight on sharpening your attention won't stop there. We will drill down toward identifying this phenomenon's more hidden, elemental causes. At some points in this journey, you will feel like you are shining a light onto the dark side of the moon as you begin to see into the core of inattention's more hidden, elemental—internal—causes.

Building on that, I will help you find ways to clear these and a plethora of other attention killers—internal and external. You will simultaneously install positive attention-building patterns into your daily routines. In short, you will rebuild your brain with whole new, high-speed, accurate attentional circuits, customized to meet your personal daily and long-range specs. The best news is that there is no ceiling to how sharp you can train your attention. I promise you a whole new and richer workplace experience for yourself, beginning today.

THE INTENTION OF THIS BOOK

The 12 Rules of Attention is intended to show you one thing: how to self-regulate and train your brain's attentional mechanism for faster and more accurate, high-quality performance at the workplace. You will learn what good attention is, what messes it up, and how to strengthen it to avoid screwups at work and guide you toward greater excellence and happiness in your professional and personal life. The good news is that you don't have to have a PhD or an MD to begin your training program. Just knowing the basics will make a big difference. Remember, there is no ceiling to how sharp and fast you can train your power of attention to be.

1

Do You Speak My Language?

Rule #1

Talk to your brain. Tell it you want it to pay attention to how *you are paying attention.*

Let's start with two common workplace examples. An everyday experience caused Jack, a data collection specialist, to wonder about how he is actually paying attention to the information he receives. His job requires him to attend a departmental meeting every Monday at 3:00 p.m. in a room that's located in a distant corner of the bottom floor of his building, about as far from his fifth-floor office as it gets. A routine email reminder goes out first thing each week to all department members. One Monday, Jack noticed that his meeting had been moved to a different location. As 3:00 p.m. approached, he was reviewing a PDF that he needed to send out by the day's end. With 15 minutes to go, he quit the PDF to ensure he'd have plenty of time to get to his meeting. He slung his computer bag over his shoulder, picked up an armful of paperwork with one hand, and grabbed his coffee with the other. Halfway to the meeting room, he wished he'd left the coffee behind; it was all getting to be too much to juggle. When he arrived, he found the door locked. It took a moment to register. He put things down and reread the morning's department email. *"Of course,"* he now recalled, *"The meeting room has been changed."* In fact, the meeting had been relocated to a room just seconds down the hall from his own office. Alone in the hallway, Jack let slip a mouthful of curses. He regrouped and stressed his way back to where he had started, thinking, *"What on earth is going on in my head?"*

On the other side of town, Susan, a real estate broker, was driving across town to meet potential clients at an open house. She stopped at a red light with her foot on the brake, feeling pleasantly relaxed—for once. Suddenly, cars on the other side of the traffic light began to drive forward, so she slowly accelerated as well. Almost immediately, the oncoming drivers blasted their horns. Like Jack, it took her a moment to realize what was happening. Checking her rearview mirror, she saw that all the other cars that had been idling behind hers were still stopped for the light on their side of the traffic signal, which was still red. A little voice in her head exclaimed, "Wow, you better get with it, girlfriend!" *"So much for my relaxing day,"* she thought.

Technically speaking, neither of these incidents was necessarily the result of inattention or distraction. They are more about *how* each individual was paying attention. If you are human, these types of screwups happen. It's not just a human thing either. They happen to small and large animals and even to devices like smoke detectors that trigger false alarms, cell phones that suddenly send messages to who knows who (mine once called 911 and landed two state police cars in my driveway), and an array of other devices engineered with AI (artificial intelligence). Who hasn't had Siri, Alexa, or Cortana, awesome as they are, pull up a truly bizarre hunk of information based on how they inputted your request? Sometimes it's downright comical. The difference is that they don't ruminate about it as we do. But still.

In the cases of Jack and Susan, their attentional machinery experienced a little blip. The systems were on per se. But they were not strategically on—that is, the *spotlight* of their attention wasn't zeroing in on the right thing. To do that, more thoughtful selectivity of detail is required. This is referred to as *selective attention*—intentionally selecting the target of your attention. (As an example, pick any word in this paragraph and intentionally zero in on it. It's like that.) Instead, both Jack and Susan were operating on automatic pilot. When this happens, all settings, input, and responses are being made and directed <u>for</u> you rather than <u>by</u> you. What's more, all three are automatic and fast—they trigger in milliseconds—and they remain unconscious to you as they "do their thing." Our practice of Rule # 1 (talk to your brain; tell it you want it to pay attention to *how* you are paying attention) alerts you that your attention is in automatic mode.

In psychology, automatic circuits are called *automatizations*. In fact, most of your daily behaviors are triggered automatically. The brain, in these cases, is doing what brains do. It's just being a brain. However, like friends who are trying to do what they think is best for you, this doesn't always work out in your best interests. The result is that, no matter how intelligent you are, you experience mind tricks of one sort or another. You think, *"Got to get to Monday's meeting"* (or your own version of that scenario in your workday), and your brain typically sets its "GPS" unconsciously and at lightning speed to accommodate, choosing your most habitual route for getting there. These are conditioned and automatized responses communicated from one neuron to another, embedded, saved, and ready to fire every time your brain thinks you need them. When they start sparking away, you virtually act, think, and feel—automatically. If you're thinking that sounds rather robotic, it is. For better or worse, it's the way we are made, and most of the decisions we make all day long come about this way. There is no reason to demonize these lightning-fast, robot-like responses. It's just the way we're built. In coming chapters I will expand on some essential and creative uses, as well as the virtues and vices of these remarkable, automatized, high-speed circuits. The more you learn to regulate them, the more you will rely on and enjoy them.

So again, when things are going okay for us, we don't give our attention machinery much thought. We are wired to feel in control. Like Jack and Susan, we begin to wonder what's up only when things go south. So although there are a myriad of reasons *not* to wait for a flub-up, including interest in peaking our game, we usually do wait. At that point, our motivation is often to avoid future trouble. The real problem is that we can tell ourselves a gazillion times to pay *more* attention, but the same hassles will just keep happening. This is because until we send our brain the message that we are taking over as its chief officer and are going to monitor as well as regulate it, it will push all the buttons for us automatically—just not always the right or best ones. When we tell our brain we want it to pay attention to *how* we are paying attention, we indicate that we intend to get involved in its decisions. This means we'll be monitoring when, where, how, and to what intensity our attentional beam is firing.

You may be surprised to discover that talking to your brain is easy. It's a good listener. However, it will erase what you say pretty quickly to (1) protect you from information overload, which it's supposed to do; and (2) get rid of what it thinks is unimportant information so it can conserve energy and put that energy to use where you most need it. This is not a big deal, though, as you can simply intercede by sending it an alternate message by using one of its favorite forms of messaging: repetition. **Your brain loves repetition and is built to pay attention to it.**

In fact, you can use repetition to cue your brain on

information that *you* think is important and don't want erased, including details you want it to retain longer and more deeply. And it will facilitate pretty cooperatively. You want your brain to put its attention on what color the traffic light is instead of some other, more extraneous, detail; you can train this response until color becomes its default focus. It's not that difficult.

TRY THIS!

I recommend using this little brain-talk activity right before significant elements in your workday. I call it the *self-scan*. The self-scan identifies details that *should* be within your attentional spotlight, keeps you from being overwhelmed by unnecessary information, and prevents vital attentional circuits from shutting down and dulling your attentional lamp. It helps you inventory what's happening in your head when you are paying attention and what's not.

Start by taking a nice slow breath and relaxing. Think of your attention as a spotlight. Select where you will aim it. Next, ask yourself these questions.

- Where am I at this moment?
- What am I trying to do?
- What *should* I be trying to do in this situation?
- What do others think I should be doing in this situation?
- What are the demands of my environment (e.g., distracters that need to be avoided, a large room that requires the need to listen more closely to hear, etc.)?
- What have I done in similar situations in the past?
- Do I want to do anything differently?
- If so, how?

Finally, proceed.

Take your time with this exercise; don't worry about speed. It will come. The more you practice, the quicker it will go. Athletes, first responders, and military personnel use similar models to get their head in the right place almost instantaneously as well as to learn very complicated movements and techniques until they start kicking in at very high speed without having to think about it. By the end of this book, you'll be able to do this too. Here's a hint: you just need a bit more information on automatizations and their potential. This aspect of attention training is so important, we'll discuss these capabilities further in upcoming chapters.

I suggest doubling down with repetition. This will help embed the scan in your mind and make it automatic. It will also transfer the scanning process to other workday activities, helping you better spotlight them in the same way. To achieve this, I recommend putting your cell phone to work and taking a picture of these questions. Placing them on your cell phone or notepad will allow you to review them as you need until the procedure becomes ingrained in your head.

REFLECTION

Reflection, which refers to visualizing or thinking over specifics of a scenario after the fact, is yet another language that brains love and respond to favorably. I highly recommend using reflection in combination with a self-scan. This approach works best immediately after a targeted work situation and again later to help you review selective parts of your workday. Doubling up gives you more control and a brighter spotlight. Reflection allows you to tweak or delete existing behavioral responses as well as develop completely new ones. Both Jack and Susan from our previous examples would benefit from this activity.

Reflection can also expose automatizations that are responsible for your behaviors. When you view your actions in retrospect, you can more easily see if they were triggered automatically or if you consciously selected them. You can also envision the way you want things to go the next time such an event presents itself. By repeating the scenario with the new (preferred) behavior a few times in your mind, you will begin the job of ingraining the situation and behavior into your long-term memory. As you reflect, you can add anything you'd do differently next time. As far as your brain is concerned, it doesn't matter if you practice your selected behavioral response in your mind or in an actual daily event. It will listen and start following your changes. You just need to talk to it, and you can make it happen. Reflection helps you get good and be good fast.

Use this technique often. Remember, repetition is one of your brain's favorite languages. Talk to your brain. It will process and store selected edited behaviors for future use. Then, when the next opportunity presents itself in real time, your brain will deliver.

PEEKING AT YOUR ATTENTION CIRCUITS

A little understanding of what goes on upstairs when your attention circuits are firing goes a long way in being able to talk to your brain. Let's take a peek.

Psychologists define attention as what (data) you are putting in your *working memory* (fast, short-term memory bank) to activate procedures to achieve imminent goals. Although there are several different elements in our attention's chain of command, here we are referring primarily to selective attention.

Your brain's attentional system is an electrochemical mechanism. It operates like an ultrasophisticated fetching system, targeting a piece of information, bringing it into your working memory, and connecting it to other information you have stored there to create processes to accomplish tasks. Your mechanism for selective attention gives you say in which details to regard and which to ignore. All of this activity takes place in the soft, grayish tissues of your brain. There are no actual pictures or maps or numbers inside there, only the crackling *trrtt-trrrttt-tttt* sounds of electrical impulses that are the voices of your neurons (brain cells) talking to each other (in sounds like fast sizzle snaps) awash in a cascade of neurochemicals, which among other things are making you feel a certain way from moment to moment—for instance, content, excited, anxious, calm. The feelings may express themselves in your mind as "This responsibility is a nuisance," "This duty is exactly what I've been waiting for," and so forth. These sparks and chemicals make up how your workday is experienced, conducted, felt, recorded, and remembered. For example, let's say a colleague pops into your office when you are smack in the middle of a phone call. How you react (to both parties) will be determined either by your automatic or by your regulated attentional functions. It's easy for your tone in such a situation to automatically get edgy. But you can, as the result of learning from past situations, catch yourself and engender softer tones instead.

Ultimately, your brain is trying to help you with tasks it thinks you want to accomplish. In Jack's example, he wanted to get to his weekly department meeting. Based on long-standing patterns, his brain quickly fetched out the details and set him on his habitual path. However, although he had received notification that the location was different, his brain hadn't registered the information well enough to retain it. As indicated, a self-scan by Jack upon receipt of the information and before the action would likely have made the difference. In Susan's example, later reflecting on the action with edits and repetition would help identify and weaken the dysfunctional automatized circuits and eventually replace them.

Take a moment now to consider a few similar examples from your own workday experiences. See if you can discover what triggered the incorrect action and consider how you could do things differently next time around.

YOUR MIND'S BEST TRICK

As we've discussed, your behaviors, daily decisions, feelings, and a bundle of personal and professional errors are significantly shaped by unconscious processes. This makes your job of paying attention to how you are paying attention interesting and sometimes tricky, because your mind *wants* you to think you're in full control so it can secretly remain behind the wheel. As we noted, your brain wants to discard what it considers unimportant so it can alert you to potential dangers and conserve its energy to protect you from potential harm. Basically, it wants to channel its energy for decisions about fight or flight and imminent tasks.

Part of talking to your brain will include identifying the unconscious triggers that will actually drive your behavior unless you become aware of them and change them. Benjamin Libet, who worked as a neuropsychologist at the University of California SF, conducted some compelling tests in the 1980s that consistently proved the power of these triggers. Libet showed time and time again how the brain uses unconscious triggers to make your decisions before you actually consciously decide on them yourself.

To prove his point, Libet's experiments engaged volunteers to perform a simple task like pressing a button or flexing their wrist. He asked the volunteers to use a timer to note the moment they were consciously aware of their decision to perform the movement. EEG sensors attached to their head monitored their brain activity. Tests showed there was unconscious brain activity initiating the action an average of half a second (and oftentimes more) before the participants decided for themselves. This may not sound like a lot, but the point is made. Libet's experiment reversed a long-held idea on mental causation: the brain and body act only *after* the mind decides.[1]

Consider this example. You call a client about a sensitive matter but she is not there, so, trying to take control of the situation, you are quick to leave a voicemail message—as if it were *your* original decision to call her up and do just that. What Libet revealed is that it is really the brain calling these shots and then we actually think about it around half a second or so later. Ever feel that a required work-training activity was a total waste of time? Can these feelings also be the result of conclusions being decided for you rather than by you? The answer is yes. All of the time? No, not always, but more times than most people think.

David Wegner, a social psychologist known for his contributions to topics of conscious will, insisted that such illusions of control are the mind's best trick.[2] We "think" we willed an action, but no. As Libet proved, far more often than we realize, we react like Siri, following a command (in this case, from our brain). Going back to the voicemail example, without regulation, it is more likely that an electrochemical reaction in your skull (unconscious to you) determined that you leave the client a voicemail message, not your conscious self. Who hasn't left a quick voice message or been sharp with a customer, client, superior, or subordinate and regretted that behavior within moments? Who hasn't thought, with regret, *"Why oh why did I just do that?"*

Consider how many work decisions you make this way daily—thoughtless, unmonitored acts that determine important daily results and ignite your feelings. If your mind is already made for you when you flex your wrist, as Libet demonstrated, what about other, more significant behaviors? For example, were you and your life partner first attracted to each other this way? What about your decision to pursue one career over another, one employer over another? What about individuals you have hired or fired, the part of the country where you chose to live, decisions about if you should marry, and so on? What can be done (if anything) to gain real control? Is real control even possible? These questions are psychologically legit.

At the core, such attentional failures are not the result of cell phones, computer games, or stock market apps making us err. I'm sorry, but the blame cannot be sourced out—not for me, you, or anyone else. Such attentional blips are not the fault of technology. The core cause goes much deeper, and it is organic. Like it or not, it's us.

The good news? This can all start to change as soon as you begin asking your brain to pay attention to how it is paying attention.

SIRI, ALEXA, CORTANA, AND YOU

Okay, so we all have the capacity to act like robots. But again, remember that there are some good aspects to this. So before we get to a few additional exercises that will help provide some immediate relief and regulation, let me indulge you with this lighthearted story of an attentional bug that could happen to any of us.

One evening, an acquaintance of mine shopped for some groceries. After he checked out he saw a friend, and they chatted for quite a while. The next morning, he looked for his groceries but couldn't find them anywhere in the house. He searched his car, anxiously reviewing in his mind what items required refrigeration. His mind then focused on the conversation he'd had with his friend. Had he left the groceries in the shopping cart where they had stood chatting? With that image in his head, he took "control" of the matter. He drove back to the store, showed them his grocery receipt, and asked if anyone had found the items. No one had, but they let him grab all of the products on his list again, at no charge, which he considered more than decent. Later that day, his wife discovered the original groceries in the back seat of *her* car. At last he recalled that he had taken her car, not his, the night before. However since this was unusual, his focus had automatically been to look for the groceries in his own car, which concurred with his usual habit.

It's easy for things like this to happen. Once they are in motion and building an experience, we believe we are in control of our thinking, logic, and behaviors. But so often we are not. In fact, we are being played like a piece of sequenced electronic music. Every note is being played for us. No one is exempt from situations like this.

Whether it's overcommitting yourself when you start a new position, running off to a meeting on automatic pilot, or losing your groceries, the dysfunctional attentional hardware is the same. It would be ridiculous to try to pay attention to every single detail that presents itself, but you can zero in on the important details by more regularly monitoring your attention, reflecting, and resetting of unconscious attention triggers together to converge toward a solution. Start today.

 Get good and be good. Talk to your brain. Tell it you want it to pay attention to how you are paying attention.

CHAPTER EXERCISES

Establish a Baseline

This exercise will help you identify the strength of your attentional spotlight. By catching yourself when you have good attention, you will better understand what it feels like. This will help you establish your personal baseline for good attention. In the future, you will be able to recognize how far away or spot on you are to your baseline, so you can begin to self-regulate adjustments as needed.

1. Start by focusing on anything in your environment or preferably a task at work.
2. Ask yourself, "How sharp is my attention at this moment?"
3. Rate your attentional sharpness as follows.
    1 star: Scattered/mind wandering
    2 stars: Energy needs to be altered considerably, too dull/ tired to pay attention or too excited to pay attention
    3 stars: Can pay attention but energy needs to be tweaked up or down
    4 stars: Attention and energy are good
    5 stars: Attention and energy are excellent, sharp, and fast
4. Jot this rating down in a notepad. Include date, day, time, location, and work task. This will be the beginning of your baseline.
5. Repeat the exercise again a few more times during the day. See if your ratings are higher or lower. Consider what changed so that you begin to see what

elements (internal or external) as well as tasks are having an impact on your attention. Make a note of these elements.

You will use this baseline information in coming chapters. You can benefit from trying this activity on a few different days. I'd like you to establish baselines that show when your attention is in a low-, mid-, or high-quality range so that you know what each of these feels like and its effects on workplace activities. As we add attention-boosting techniques in coming chapters, you can use your baseline to identify when you need them, what effect you are trying to achieve, and which to apply.

Self-Scans and Reflection

If you are not already using this chapter's self-scan in combination with reflection, this is a good time to start. Go back and reread these sections on pages 5 and 6. I recommend starting out slowly. Pick one activity to try out these techniques per day (or over a few days) until you get used to the process.

2

Know Your Mindware

Rule #2

Awareness, mindfulness, and attention are not the same thing. Use each individually to strengthen the others and significantly lighten up and improve the way you perform and feel.

Keeping an unburdened mind-set sounds good to most of us as we traverse the workday. The more we can keep the wind in our sails and avoid any turbulence the better. Yet no doubt you have found that at times your day moves less fluidly. Believe it or not, uncontrolled attention has a lot to do with the way this cookie crumbles. Regulation, on the other hand, will get you closer to the lighter, more effortless, flowing mind-set you desire. A little knowledge of how you can integrate awareness, mindfulness, and attention to form a powerful psycho-physical team will get you there. Let's look.

Consider the following simulation: You are at work waiting for a scheduled 10:00 a.m. phone call. The call is important, so much so that you spent time the night before prepping talking points. Now you've gone in to work early to crystallize things in your mind. Ten o'clock comes and goes. But nada, non, rien. At around 10:30 your phone rings. It's the call. You answer pleasantly. However, you detect an apologetic, hurried tone from your caller. At lightning speed (literally, milliseconds) in the unconscious quarters of your head, your mind is updating incoming details—computing the tone you just perceived and streaming it to a mental (neural) data collection on this and similar experiences you've had. These new links will create your next responses. Their file is continuously updating. It will serve as a resource for future experiences and trigger how you act and feel during those situations. You have trillions of these connections in your mind. Each is a possible response template that will shape experiences to come. If, like most people, you let these mental templates fire old habits without your conscious "say," they will. And afterward you'll have to live with or deal with the outcome. Remember, nature has made you this way to help you deal with information overload as well as to help you use your mental energy efficiently. If you want to purposefully step up and change anything, self-regulation will be your way.

Let's get back to the tone you noticed in your caller's voice when you picked up the phone. You can already read the writing on the wall. It says, "*There's a problem* and the caller is sorry but..." Suddenly you feel all your preparation about to backfire. Your mind is going places you didn't expect, sending you messages that you are about to veer off on the wrong foot. It might be a quick feeling. Perhaps it's a voice you hear in your head that becomes bellicose and fires a mental pejorative at the individual who is causing your disappointment, or it warns you, "Be careful." Whichever, your response is about to kick in. Then— surprise!—the other shoe drops and your caller inserts that he is unable to do the call at all right now. He offers to call you back at 5:00 p.m. and asks if that's okay.

SURPRISE, SURPRISE

Of course it's not okay. You were appreciably ready, willing, and able when the initial time to connect with the client arrived.

We have all had similar experiences. In cases such as this, your mind's natural ability to make constant predictions from incoming details influences the quality and outcome of your experience. This amazing predictive network is associated with your brain's awareness and attentional systems. It is key to managing your daily activities. What's more, the mental files that this brain machinery draws upon to make such predictions are constantly updating, ingraining new links into your memory. These new links, often invisibly, influence the way you pay attention. They manipulate the way you respond to your imminent and longer-range goals, including immediate work tasks and even career changes down the line.

Mind you, nobody is saying these response hacks, which occur naturally, have to be good—or bad. They can, however, determine if you'll hit the ball out of the park or strike out before you even get to the plate. Whether you succeed or mess up will have a lot to do with how you integrate each of these machines. Awareness of the speaker's tone in the phone call incident serves as an example. It makes what the caller will say next a little less surprising and more predictable. This seems like a small detail, but it provides you with an essential foot ahead. It helps guide your focus to a response that can be advantageous. It also doubles to strengthen your attention to behaviors that could mess you up. All this helps you more easily avoid such errors. Most of us do not separate the networks of awareness, mindfulness, and attention in our tool chest of mental resources. In doing so, however, you can begin to regulate them. You can increase their strength and efficacy. Let's look closer.

TO EXPECT OR NOT TO EXPECT

Evolution gifted us with the ability to predict. As part of our fight or flight mechanisms, it helped us predict existential detail in our environments. Without it we would have become an easy lunch for predators. As a result, we evolved to respond to subtler detail around us without having to think much about it. We learned that a specific scent, a batch of leaves rustling just so, or a brief shadow could provide a hint of what could happen next. This sensitivity made us faster and more proficient at taking care of ourselves.

There has been a plethora of exciting attention studies on the role of predictability and nonpredictability, because there is a lot we can do with these circuits. These circuits allow your brain to keep track of what it has experienced (and how often), adapt to regularities, and forecast upcoming details based on recent context. They also allow you to detect and update links to include surprising details and react to and update the unexpected (so it is less unexpected next time around) if predictions have gone wrong.[1]

Psychologically, the more times a specific action occurs from a certain set of details, the more you grow to expect it. So, going back to our opening example, the more times you have already experienced such a call or a similar sudden change in timing with a colleague, a client, or a superior, the more likely you will use information you've saved in memory. Just remember, your brain will save this information whether you are conscious of it or not. This can be good or bad—depending on what you've saved and how you apply it. The more you can make yourself able to recognize such links, the more you will be able to control them—that is, keep them around or eliminate them.

Without regulation, your mind will usually respond to the

salient (attention-grabbing) details in memory that are vying for its attention. You may be aware of some of these but others—emotional and otherwise—will remain unconscious to you. What I am saying is this: *you need to develop, execute, and act on your sense of awareness.* Remember that fleeting moment in the example when the caller's tone seemed apologetic? Missing that kind of detail in real time could be catastrophic. Your mind would likely get hijacked by the ingrained, automatic behaviors you've already stored in your head just for times like this, and if your pattern from past situations is to fly off the hook, then you run the risk of automatically doing that yet again with no conscious say in it.

Physiologically, these behavioral circuits fire so fast you might think, *"What chance do I have to take this bull by the horns?"* But I assure you, in the chapters to come you will develop quite a few strategies that will make a big dent in defeating knee-jerk reactions and ultimately help you keep your workday looking a lot prettier.

Let me give you a personal example. As a young academic, I ran into a veteran professor who had developed a reputation as a real jokester. She used to come up with some (ahem) truly memorable, though I should say nonendorsable, methods of problem solving. This is one I can share.

At certain times of the year, the academics could count on a long line at every photocopying machine in the house. Right before finals, I found myself running from one photocopier to another to another because all of the lines were huge. I jetted to the basement, where there was one last machine to check out, but a sign on that copier said "Out of Order." When I hiked back to the third floor, that line had actually increased. I finally flew back down to the basement, thinking I'd play my last card and try fixing the machine myself.

Guess what? There was a veteran professor at the machine, photocopying away—with no problem. The scene didn't immediately register until she looked at me, pointed to the sign, and placed her index finger over her lip. "Shhh," she said, grinning from ear to ear. She'd scammed everybody because we all "expected" the machines to be down due to the high demand.

After that, whenever I saw the sign, I had a private chuckle and anticipated that the machine would be functional. My awareness of what had happened previously would instantly click in. One time, though, I saw a sign that read "Not in Service," and, in fact, the machine didn't work. After that I realized I would have to distinguish between her signs (by the wording and lettering) and those posted by the technicians. And my mind added that link to its files so I'd be able to tell the difference.

People with pets can relate to the same principle. They expect their pet will be hungry in the morning and afternoon, and they learn to anticipate their pet's routine method of indicating mealtimes. The day the pet acts differently often sparks their concern over the pet's health, especially if it is getting on in years.

Expectation runs in your mind all day long. At times it is at the forefront of your thoughts, such as when you are expecting a call at a scheduled time or a task to be completed in a certain way. Other times your expectation is running in the background, such as when you expect your children to be waiting at the usual spot, at the usual time, when you are picking them up after school. Similarly, you may immediately expect the dreaded person at work who doesn't know when to "button up" to interrupt you whenever you cross paths and make you late for wherever you're headed. Anticipation can also be more distant; you may expect to take your summer vacation in July or receive a promotion after two years. Sometimes anticipation is almost unconscious, like when you expect to hear a ring tone after you have dialed a number on your cell phone. *Importantly, the amount of surprise you feel parallels the amount of predictability you anticipate, and this is connected to your awareness network.*

If your phone suddenly turns off after dialing, you may be only slightly surprised. You don't freak out because you've experienced this before when the phone was out of power, and you know you forgot to power it up recently. You're aware, and it's ingrained and computing into your experience.

However, have you ever picked up the phone to place a call and then, without any ring tone at all, you've heard that person's voice on the other end—only to discover they were calling you? Now that's a surprise. (The intensity would depend on how many times this has happened in your past.) What if, after dialing, your phone suddenly displayed an unsavory YouTube video in a language you do not know? Your surprise would be greater. Again, all this would depend on previous experiences. Is it a malfunction in your settings? A hack? Is your phone toast? Whatever you would do, think, or feel would be largely determined by how well you can maneuver your mindwares of awareness, mindfulness, and attention. So let's take a deeper look.

AWARENESS

Imagine, for a moment, we are in an auditorium. I am in front beginning a talk on attention training. I have a PowerPoint presentation on a screen. I am using a handheld remote to change slides. Some people see the remote, some don't. Now I am walking to the back of the room. I ask you not to follow me with your eyes. Instead I ask you to pick out any one of four pictures currently on the screen and look closely at its details. Once in back, I stand for a moment in silence. Then I ask you if you still think I am in the room. Everyone, of course, answers, "Yes." I ask, "Did you know I was there before I said anything?" Again, everyone answers, "Yes." It's no different than if you are reading a book at home. You know where you are; you don't have to keep checking. You may know that your partner is watching television in the next room. This is awareness, a consciousness that extends beyond the periphery of your attentional spotlight, and you have it at your disposal. Often, however, you simply aren't aware that you are aware. In attention training, our job is to discover more ways to use this machine to our advantage.

When driving, you can be aware, for instance, of a hairpin turn coming up in two miles and yet focus your attention on navigating through traffic directly ahead. As you drive, details become available to you that the turn is imminent. Your brain's awareness mechanism almost instantly calibrates your attention to focus on the turn.

Expectation, predictability, and surprise are all influenced by your awareness. Because you are aware of certain details, you may be surprised if something different from what your expectations are set for occurs. You are less surprised (or maybe not at all surprised) if you are able to accurately predict from the details. Your ability to attend advantageously toward goals is also affected by these variables. Later in this chapter you will see why and how you can use this predisposition throughout the day to more effortlessly hit your goals and keep your good vibes flowing.

MINDFULNESS

Mindfulness can be understood as largely relating to energy. In this way, mindfulness itself is nonreactive to whatever you're observing. Think about this: mindfulness is not just about being present. Rather, mindfulness is about increasing the energy (currency) of your presence. For example, when you give sound more presence, you are making it crisper and sharper, of higher definition. The energy of mindfulness does that for your experiences. Think of increasing the brightness on your cell phone flashlight by sliding the brightness bar upward to a stronger setting. Similarly, increasing your presence by boosting its energy (mindfulness) will sharpen your focus. When your focus feels too mellow, use your mindfulness mechanism to boost it.

TRY THIS!

Take a moment and try this simple mindful-breathing activity, which is a quick way to boost mindfulness.

1. Make yourself aware of your breathing.
2. As you breathe a little deeper and slower, notice the slight jump in your energy.
3. Begin to experience this with each breath.
4. Mentally insert (direct) that jump of energy (no matter how tiny) into wherever your attention is aimed.

These energy spikes will also sharpen details in your field of awareness, so you get two for the price of one.

Continue the breathing exercise and, as you do, read this paragraph again:

Mindfulness can be understood as largely relating to energy. In this way, mindfulness itself is nonreactive to whatever you're observing. Think about this: mindfulness is not just about being present. Rather, mindfulness is about increasing the energy (currency) of your presence. For example, when you give sound more presence, you are making it crisper and sharper, of higher definition. The energy of mindfulness does that for your experiences. Think of increasing the brightness on your cell phone flashlight by sliding the brightness bar upward to a stronger setting. Similarly, increasing your presence by boosting its energy (mindfulness) will sharpen your focus. When your focus feels too mellow, use your mindfulness mechanism to boost it.

You should experience a slight uptick in attention—that is, in the sharpness of your focus. For use in longer activities, you can employ mindful breathing at various points throughout.

If you don't feel enough oomph from this breathing exercise, don't worry. It takes a little practice to get more juice out of it, and it alone is not going to spark any high-wattage change. However, it can certainly provide some immediate relief. Many additional tools to increase mindfulness, especially when you need more watts than this basic method generates, will be examined throughout the book.

ATTENTION

Attention, as we have defined it, is an electrochemical fetching mechanism that targets a piece of information, bringing it into your working memory and connecting it to other information you have stored there to create processes to accomplish your needs. This information can include expectations and awareness.

Attention can occur without awareness or mindfulness. Although there is still exciting work to be done in this area, many scientists have demonstrated that awareness can also occur without having to pay attention.[2] As an example, you may be working at your computer with your pet kitten sprawled out on a chair next to you. Although you are attending to what's on your computer screen, you are still conscious of the kitten on the chair. You're hardwired to handle both.

Functionally, awareness without attention helps cut down on how much of your attentional energy you are using. Remember, your supply is not endless. You may find it interesting that things you are aware of but are not specifically paying attention to can continue to bear influence on your thoughts and actions.

INTEGRATING ALL THREE MINDWARES ON THE JOB

Remember that although attention is a limited mental currency, there is no ceiling to its quality. The limitation is in how much attentional energy you can expend on a task before draining your pipeline. Nonregulation is a recipe for fatigue, flub-ups, missed opportunities, and general bad vibes. An expert martial artist once told me, "Our bodies are vessels. They can hold only a limited amount of energy, either good or bad. Our job is to empty out the bad and replace it with good."[3] We have already seen how mindfulness can energetically boost your presence when you need to be on. Making yourself aware of important information will give you an energy uptick as well. It will conserve the amount of attention you need to apply to associated tasks, and all this will increase your daily energy and generate a greater attention span. Awareness, mindfulness, and attention form a team whose coordinated effect is greater than the sum of the parts.

ACQUIRING EVEN MORE ATTENTIONAL POWER

Consider the photocopier story or the hairpin turn example. Simply making yourself aware—having a kind of peripheral realization of a certain detail that may be occurring in the background of your immediate attention—will give your focus more "glue," so to speak. It will sharpen your attention on that particular detail when it pops up in the natural course of events. News networks make hay of this concept when they display teasers of what's coming up in their broadcast in small sidebars on your TV screen. It's their way of turning on your awareness machinery, building your expectation, keeping you fixed to their channel, and, finally, rewarding you with the story when it arrives. Tying information to the body's reward system has a profound effect. In this case, when an anticipated news clip finally arrives, you'll be more glued to it—after all, you'll want your reward. Incidentally, whenever you make yourself aware of sideline information to help you remember, you are self-regulating, freeing up headspace (and page space) for other things, and increasing the odds that you will recall the information you need. When you do remember, you feel rewarded. This makes the process ingrain itself to work faster and better the next time you use it. Today's science is still turning over more stones when it comes to how awareness, mindfulness, and attention integrate and synergize, yet we can now say that without the preawareness we have been discussing, you will be inclined to spend less time on peripheral information and possibly even miss it entirely when it moves into your immediate attention. Here's an example. If you are not preaware of emergency procedures when operating a piece of equipment, you will be less attentive to the important details if you need them, even though they may be right in front of your face.

Going back to our earlier example of the rescheduled phone call, catching the speaker's tone is a peripheral detail that is significant toward successfully navigating the conversation. In the example, catching the tone enables you to better predict where the phone call is headed and gives you essential extra time to shape a response that is advantageous to you.

Here's how it works. Technically, awareness gives you more and longer salience (stick-to-it-ive-ness, or glue) to certain details. In contrast, an unaware observer sees the details but moves on to other streaming information. This all happens in milliseconds. Consequently, if you are relying on catching an important detail as it streams, you have to be incredibly lucky or have a little help in advance. The latter is what you gain with attention training.

By learning how to preset your awareness network, you can likely attach crucial information to a moment in progress and use awareness like a type of alarm clock.[4] Consider this parental mantra, "Look both ways before crossing." Although not fool-proof, this simple mantra has nonetheless spared innumerable children injury. This is, again, because the preaware person will not so easily lose touch with important sideline details when those details arise in the real-time spotlight.

Let's say you're at work in a situation of sudden changes— budget stats, rapid adjustments when operating machinery, or even within a sudden breakdown in communication with a domineering coworker. If you have preset behavioral responses to initiate guidance, then your responsivity will be more on task and will work to your advantage. Your awareness will grease your mind's infinite feelings, memories, and links, bringing them all to bear on a given situation.

The next vignette, about Maddie Peters, a flight attendant for American Airlines, reveals a lighthearted workplace flub-up with a sweet conclusion. The account highlights how expecta-tion, predictability, awareness, and attention can click in to make a better moment for all.

On this particular day, the airline's CEO, Doug Parker, was on a flight from Phoenix to Dallas. As Maddie later told report-ers, "We knew he was going to be aboard and had to be on our best behavior." However, despite her awareness, something unpredictable happened. According to the news report, as Maddie was serving beverages, "the person ahead of her in the aisle suddenly stopped and took a step backward, sending her full tray of drinks flying" and spilling half the drinks on Maddie and the rest on Doug.[5] Maddie, who'd been with the company for four years, later said she'd wanted to drop dead on the spot, noting that she'd never done anything like that before.[6] Fortunately, Doug was totally cool about it. As Maddie recounted, he "laughed it off and then visited the galley to reassure [me]. When [I] asked him, 'Am I fired?' he said, 'Of course not.'"[7]

Maddie's response of being mortified is easy to understand and relate to. We've been there, done that. Because she'd never spilled anything on anyone before, she had no links in her mental repertoire telling how to respond from there. Links that were clicking off were likely being triggered by prompts to be on her best that day.

What I love about this story is that accidents do happen, but Doug's response is also admirable and worth noting. For starters, humor is a great way to disengage bad vibes. It changes your own blood chemistry to something less alarming and more calming and upbeat. It can also do the same for others. His measured response helped cool off a potentially escalating moment. What's more, it profiles him as a good guy, steady and compassionate. A leader. And of course, for him as well as for Maddie, useful positive details gleaned from the experience were updated in their memories. These new links (including using humor) will likely spark empathetic reactions in the future from both individuals.

Was there anything Maddie could have done in advance to prevent the incident? Unlikely. As the old saying goes, "Experience is the best teacher." However, any time setbacks happen to you, you can quicken the learning process and ingrain it by practicing reflection, as we've discussed earlier.

ATTENTION CAN WOBBLE

"Take away awareness and attention should start to wobble," notes psychologist Michael Graziano, who designed an experiment to test this prediction.[8] During the test, study participants look at a screen, and every few seconds the researcher flashes a dot. Sometimes the participants notice the dot and sometimes they miss it. Every time the dot is flashed, the researcher measures the amount of attention given to it. Graziano hypothesized that if you are preaware of the dot, then it should snag more of your attention when it appears in front of you again. As a result, your attention "should spike right after the dot appears, stabilize on the dot for a while, and fade after maybe a half second. If you're unaware of the dot, it should still snag your attention, but then the attention paid to the dot should fluctuate, just like a faulty machine when the control model is missing."[9]

In Graziano's experiement participants without awareness of the dot didn't pay any less attention to it. Their attention, however, wobbled. However, preawareness steadied their attentional beam and gave it more stick-to-it-ive-ness to a specifically targeted detail—in this case the dot.[10] Sometimes that kind of preset extra attentional oomph can make all the difference!

TRY THIS!

Activate your awareness and your mind's ability to predict scenarios. This can boost your attention and task performance at work.

1. Start by identifying two important tasks you engage in often during the day or week. Jot down on a card or your notebook one or two tasks where circumstances or

    details may change quickly as you proceed (e.g., taking
    phone calls, responding to certain emails, interpersonal
    exchanges, using electronics, etc.).

2. Jot down the purpose of the task (e.g., why you are performing it, why it's important to you, why it's important
   to others, what you expect, what others expect, etc.).
3. Note the two most important details toward successfully handling the task that you should be aware of
   before engaging in it. Be specific.
4. Read your account during breakfast and also randomly
   as the week progresses.

You can also create corresponding icons for the items and post
them on your cell phone. This way you can quickly review them
a few times randomly as well as before your activity. I recommend using both the list and the icons.

PAYING ATTENTION WITHOUT
BEING AWARE

Your brain can also pay attention to things it doesn't see. Po-Jang
Hsieh, PhD, of the Duke-NUS Neuroscience and Behavioral
Disorders Research Program, and colleagues suggest that evolution could have brought about this brain capacity as a survival
mechanism (e.g., unconsciously realizing there's a predator in
the bushes before being aware of it). This comes from a need to
direct our attention to details of possible interest even before we
are able to become aware of them.[11]

    The phenomenon was further highlighted by cognitive neu-
roscientist Sheng He of the University of Minnesota and his colleagues, who demonstrated that invisible images of naked males
caught the attention of women, and undetectable pictures of naked

females captured the attention of men.[12] Such subliminal images are capable of bearing their influence on people's focus even after they are canceled out. According to the research, "Over the course of 32 trials, men were significantly better at detecting the orientation of Gabor patches [abstract shapes] when they appeared in the slot formerly occupied by an invisible image of a nude woman."[13] Such nudity-driven focusing worked almost as well for women, as long as the image accorded with their sexual preference."[14]

Many related studies have also been conducted in this area. Hsieh and his colleagues, for example, further tested the concept of attention without awareness with an experiment that used the occurrences of visual pop-outs. Each participant was set up with a display that showed a different video to each eye. One eye was shown colorful, shifting patterns and all awareness went to that eye, which is consistent with the way the brain works. The other eye was shown a pattern of shapes that didn't move. Most were green, but one was red. Then subjects were tested to see what part of the screen their attention went to. The researchers found that people's attention went to that red shape—even though they had no idea they'd seen it at all.[15] This supports the suggestion that we are wired with a capacity to be able to direct attention to objects even before becoming aware of them.

In another experiment, however, the researchers found that if people were distracted with a demanding task, the red shape didn't attract their attention unconsciously anymore— supporting the idea that you need a certain amount of energy to pay attention to something even if you aren't aware of it.[16] Following this reasoning, a demanding task at work can offer a way to regulate the power of your focus. Think of daily work-day brain-hijacks like depression, fears and anxieties, or unexpected negative circumstances. Your attention can follow these distractions without your conscious knowledge of it occurring, and they can hijack your attention and flow in a current task.

In cases like these, *a push-the-pedal-to-the-metal task may be just what you need to get you out of your funk at work.* In fact, sometimes you don't even need to "know" what's got you stuck in the mud. Ramping up your engagement with a current task (or switching tasks if you can) may jet you out of a bad place and into something prettier. You can also add frosting to the cake by supplementing with after-work activities that take you well out of your comfort zone and going all out on them. I recommend activities like mountain biking, rock climbing, hiking, a new course at the gym, dance, martial arts, or power yoga. These work great to help clear your headspace, increase your positive energy, and provide deeper relief! Sometimes altering your state of mind just a quarter turn is all you need.

TRY THIS!

Discovering where the mind is at can be fun. Next time you get off an elevator or leave a café or bus, consider some of the individuals who were in the space with you. What do you recall most about them? A face? An article they are carrying? A piece of clothing? Trace the footsteps of your thoughts and feelings. Why was your attention attracted to these specific details? Your answers may be amusing and will likely reveal some of what's occurring unconsciously in your head that is also affecting your thoughts, feelings, and performance.

SELF-AWARENESS

Most of us aren't often checking in with the captain of our ship, the person we are on the inside, to get a take on how things are going. Aside from that little voice commenting, "Darn, I should have done that differently," or "Man, I wish the boss wouldn't bark orders at me all day long," we often lack self-awareness. I recommend carving out some space to slow down every now and then just to check in with yourself.

Plenty of research shows that keeping a self-aware brain can make constructive willful change possible at your workplace. One such study conducted by researchers from Cornell University's School of Industrial and Labor Relations found that leadership searches didn't put enough weight on self-awareness. Nonetheless, research results showed that self-awareness should be a top criterion in seeking awesome business leaders. In fact, researchers emphasized that "a high self-awareness score was the strongest predictor of overall success."[17] Whether you are already in a position of leadership, aspiring toward one, or just looking to improve your game, self-awareness is at the heart of all improvement—including making your attention work to your greatest advantage.

According to Korn Ferry Institute, a global organizational consulting firm, companies benefit too. Their research shows a correlation between self-awareness in their leaders and their overall financial performance.[18]

Make no mistake, self-awareness is your headquarters for success. It will guide you to deep personal and interpersonal satisfaction both on the job and off. But what exactly is this coveted brain machine?

Self-awareness is another type of awareness. Specifically, it is your ability to peek into your own mind with understanding. In doing so, you are able to look at how your awareness, mindfulness, and attention machines are operating internally. This allows you to listen to your thoughts, feelings, dreams, beliefs, memories, motivations, and even blood chemistry changes, such as the feeling of a peripheral burst of adrenaline or the euphoric vibe of endorphins. Self-awareness allows you to monitor who you have been, who you are today, and who you want to be in the future. As you alter your attention by toggling back and forth between these internal self-pages and your external interests and goals, you can fine-tune your actions so they are best in sync with your goals. This is your mechanism for feeling good "through and through"!

Let's say that during the late, disappointing phone call we discussed earlier, you briefly pause to practice self-awareness. First, you might quickly consider how much the contents of the call mean to your day's success at work and future goals (e.g., a new contract, which yields more money for you and your family, which can be used for further education and as a highlight for future employment). Each of these considerations might enable you to put the brakes on a potentially detrimental response and instead opt for the more favorable one (e.g., camaraderie, cooperation, and the best of you). You will be more likely to react with humor (or at least grace), as American Airlines's CEO Doug Parker did, to create a win-win.

By helping you be all that you can be, self-awareness is arguably one of your most essential engines to good attention and decision making, behavioral control, and quality living. A self-aware person knows what's good for them and how they can willfully fit into the bigger picture. They can gauge from their actions which can best lead to success and personal development and which will not. In contrast, unaware individuals can rise and fall pretty fast at the workplace, yet because they are on autopilot, they don't know why. We've all been there to some capacity. The problem is that although most people think they are self-aware, only about 10 percent to 15 percent of us actually are.[19] What if someone were to ask you, "When was the last time you knew why you were doing whatever you are doing?"[20] What would you say? Would you see the matrix of where you've been, where you are, and where you could potentially be headed? I think most of us, in a moment's private self-examination, would say we need to develop more self-awareness.

Nearly everyone gets caught in life's busyness. Work and careers have a way of fueling that. There's often no time to just think, and years of being flat out. The usual culprits are school, college, family, and employment. We get sucked into whatever the prevailing socioeconomic, institutional modus operandi is—confident that the ideas we are expressing and living by are our own, yet blindsided that we may be getting blindsided. Most of us (including me) keep promising ourselves we will "figure it all out" tomorrow. Meanwhile our peace of mind and happiness get placed on hold. All too often, tomorrow doesn't come soon enough. I'm here to tell you that we can't let that happen. And... well, it's never too late to do what we can against it.

This bears repetition: regulation relies on awareness. No one is self-aware 24/7. Nonetheless, we can train for those important, special moments and shape them with intention.

VISUALIZATION: THE GREAT ENERGY BOOSTER

Seeing yourself in an important situation in which you want to perform your best is sometimes half the battle toward accomplishing it. Visualization is an amazingly effective tool to help you. Applied to many areas of work—from athlete to military service member, from educator to first responder, from corporate worker to laborer—visualization is a mechanism that will increase your psychological currency and, specifically, your preawareness network. Remember that preawareness boosts your attentional strength and lowers your risk of missing important peripheral details, increasing your odds of responding to a sudden change in tone in a coworker's voice to your advantage or to empathetically answering the wash of emotions in another's words or catching the lack of them.

Visualization can produce new circuits in your awareness, mindfulness, and attentional machinery. Just as a tennis player might use visualization to smoothen her high-low-high swing in tennis, you can use it to feel more animated when you arrive at work in the morning or during off-hours. Through visualization, you can activate certain brain networks (language, motor, memory) and edit, short-circuit, or create new circuits for positive, advantageous behavioral responses.

Because of the brain's plasticity, you can literally remold you brain's operational system so that it is working more in accordance with your goals and desires. For this to occur, however, you need lots of repeated practice so that, in your mind's language, it gets the message.

Know your mindwares. Use each individually to strengthen other mindwares and significantly lighten up and improve the way you perform and feel.

CHAPTER EXERCISES

Making Yourself Aware in Advance

Choose a situation you'd like to improve at work. Start with something small. Ask yourself, "What about the situation is important to me? Why? What, from this situation, do I absolutely need to accomplish for myself and others?" Use your mind's eye to visualize how the activity might play out in real time. Watch yourself in the situation as if you were watching a movie. Observe your typical responses in the scenario. Ask yourself, "What responses are working? What would I like to change? How do these relate to *why* the situation is important to me? How do they relate to what I want to accomplish? What positive behavioral traits do I have in my attention tool kit that will facilitate?" Pick one or two things you want to change in your approach. Write them down on an index card and put it in your pocket. Review it randomly (not overdoing it). It may be something like "Listen more than I talk" or "Don't interrupt" or "Don't boom so much when I speak." Just focus on one or two details that you feel will swing your approach to your advantage.

Don't skimp on this next step. Briefly consider why the situation is important to you now and how it can tie in to your near goals and longer-range goals so that you know why you are strategizing the way you are. Review your index card before the activity and use its information as a prompt during the activity. You can review it again afterward and think about whether there is anything that could be tweaked in your approach.

Boosting Your Mindfulness

Building on the breathing activity on page 23, condensing physical and mental energy is a mindfulness-boosting activity that has been used in martial arts training over many years. It is intended to give you a larger lift when your energy dipstick feels low. Martial artists can generate explosive power with this approach, but you don't need to be a martial artist or in a dojo to use this tool. With practice, you can achieve fast mental and physical acuity for any workplace goal. There are a few steps, but once you carry out the activity a few times, you can go through its parts quickly so you can use it as a daily staple. You can even work it in midaction when you need a burst of energy on the spot. At other times, you may like to take a break to recharge.

1. Begin by taking a slow, deep breath, inhaling naturally through your nose and exhaling through your mouth. Try to relax different places in your body where you feel tense.
2. Visualize yourself pulling energy from your limbs and the earth below you. Visualize yourself streaming this energy—using your breaths—to stream it into your core. Then, with each breath, picture yourself condensing that energy into a smaller and smaller space, until you visualize it compressed into a tight bundle the size of a sugar cube.
3. Breathe from your belly, then exhale and picture the energy going outward like beams of light through your entire body. Feel your energy surge.

You can get creative and use your own imagery. The examples I have given are simply to give you the idea. With practice, you can learn to significantly increase this energy boost and hence your mindfulness toward whatever you're doing next.

Putting It All Together

For the sharpest results, integrate your mindwares. A good way to start is to pick one workplace task where you'd like to increase your performance. Follow the regimen in the first exercise for making yourself aware in advance, and apply it to your selected task. But before you do, follow the mindfulness-boosting techniques in the second exercise. When you combine these activities, they will bring you to a state of strong, energized awareness. Then, from the scenario you visualized, pick a single aspect of your performance that you feel would give you the most workplace bang for your buck if you could improve it. Again, ask yourself, "What positive behavioral skills do I have in my tool kit that will facilitate this?" Rerun the visualization through your mind with those skills. Repeat randomly, fine-tuning until it ingrains itself in your mind. When the situation presents itself in real time, use mindfulness to brighten your attentional beam. As discussed in this chapter, your preawareness and mindfulness will provide important support links that are already in place.

3

Your Good and Bad Zombies

Rule #3

Renovate your mind's automatizations to stay on top of your game. Your brain loves automatic triggers. You can't live without them. They make decisions easy, fast, and seemingly harmonious. Use them to your advantage.

Have you ever taken a long drive on the interstate only to arrive at your destination and suddenly realize you were zoned out for most of the ride? In these situations, you usually have little to no recollection of landmarks or even of your driving. This experience, which is actually quite common, freaks out a lot of people.

But where were you, anyway, when you were so zoned out? You were in what I call the "drone zone," operating on what is commonly referred to as *automatic pilot*. Most animals drone around like this throughout most of the day, and we humans are no exception. It's natural and the mind-set delivers a lot of good. As we discussed in chapter 1, automatizations are templates for actions, thoughts, and feelings that trigger very quickly—faster than if you had to consciously invoke them. They kick in all day long, under your radar, and you rely on them. In fact, automatizations allow you the luxury to efficiently deal with tasks that involve a hurricane of neural activity while clearing headspace to simultaneously delve—deeply even—into other areas of your concern.

Although this may sound like multitasking, it's not. Your autopilot system doesn't eat up your attentional and *cognitive energy* (mental energy) in the way that multitasking does. Instead, it guides your performance from the catacombs of your mind without your conscious involvement. And that's the point. When the conditions for which an automatization was established display themselves in your daily experiences, the preset behavior or action robotically *fires*. For example, the car in front of you slows down; you want to pass, the coast is clear, passing is legal in your lane, so you pass. You just do it. It's kind of like a set alert on your cell phone. The automatization, like the alert, won't drain much energy. It also won't inhibit your attention in the meantime, freeing you to work on whatever task or goal you are onto.

Basically, automatizations provide virtually instant neural links to behavioral responses (thoughts, feelings, actions) that you need imminently to get jobs done and that you use a lot, especially those where you don't want to be spending your mental energy thinking about, trying to remember, or learning or relearning details. Can you imagine if every time you drove your car you had to go over each step, from putting the key in the ignition to how much pressure to place on the gas pedal to what to look out for while you are pulling out of your driveway? As another example, automatization frees you to jog through a park without thinking about your athletic form or posture, which means you can enjoy the rose gardens along the way or mentally acknowledge a coworker's contagious positivity on a project you are jointly working on.

Christof Koch, PhD, is the president and chief science officer of the Allen Institute for Brain Science as well as a neurobiologist at CalTech. Koch, with his former colleague and friend Francis Crick, PhD (the same Crick of the double helix discovery fame), coined the term *zombie* to refer to such automatizations. According to Koch, they "called these unconscious mechanisms zombie agents. Collectively, this zombie army manages the fluid and rapid interplay of muscles and nerves that is at the heart of all skills and is at the heart of a lived life."[1] As you will see, some zombies are good, while others are a nuisance and still others are downright dangerous. Some do not require any conscious generation on your part, and others can be intentionally created, which means you can craft an automatized action for a specific behavior. Further, you can self-regulate your automatic action to peak performance—anything from how to improve your golf swing to how to avoid an ambush on the battlefield to how to greet grumpy customers with infectious calm. What kicks in these trained skills is the same guidance system that got you safely to your destination on the interstate—your good zombies.

You may recall Captain Chesley Sullenberger, who became famous when he and copilot Jeff Skiles landed US Air Flight 1549 on the Hudson River, saving the lives of 153 passengers, their crew, and, of course, themselves.[2] On the emergency landing's 10-year anniversary, January 2019, Captain Sullenberger described to ABC News how the plane hit a flock of Canadian geese that knocked out both engines and how he was able to maneuver the plane to land the flight on the river. As Sullenberger told it, "The stress was too intense, but we had that focus...to be able to do the job in spite of how stressful it was."[3] As far as his thoughts were concerned, the captain recalled, "I never had any extraneous thoughts in those few seconds that we had," referring to his decision to execute the water landing. "I never thought about my family. I never thought about anything other than controlling the flight path and solving each problem in turn until, finally, we had solved them all."[4]

Captain Sullenberger, a former US Air Force fighter pilot with more than 20,000 hours of flying time, continued his efforts that day even after the water landing. Before he exited, he summoned the energy to search the plane twice to make sure everyone had been evacuated.[5]

The captain's heroic landing is a good example of how past experience, strong values, and being in the present moment—even amidst incredible, incredible stress—can find adaptive solutions to tasks and result in amazing focus and positive outcomes.

HOW ZOMBIES ARE BORN

Early on, psychological work with automatizations zeroed in on matching skills required to accomplish a goal and practicing them until they become automatic. This strategy can be seen in the world of athletics or in learning an effective sales pitch or even in putting on a smile when greeting a customer and a neutral or compassionate face when meeting an anxious coworker. The general thought was that such an approach to automatization required three things: an act of will, learning, and practice. So, the process was generated via conscious effort. The concept itself, however, was nothing new.

The world of martial arts offers a good example. Dating back millennia, martial artists discovered that repetition of a technique like a block or a kick to the point of perfection could make its execution in a real-life event perfect, virtually instantaneous and consistently so. Most martial arts and yoga students (as well as dancers and all other athletes) in schools all over the world know that when they are first learning a technique, the thing that messes them up most is having to think about what they are doing while they are trying to do it. They can't wait for the day that they can act like the Nike motto: "Just do it!" One of the greatest lessons of athletic arts is that they teach you that such a day does come. The same holds true for workday behaviors you want to change, replace, or create to get better results. *The formula is simple: will it, learn how, and train it with lots of reps as you would any muscle in the gym.*

But automatic mode doesn't apply to just physical performance. Psychological and emotional states of mind can be achieved this way too. This also is nothing new. Dating from as far back as the early days of martial arts to today's athletic and military training, practices like meditation and mindfulness as well as other mind-sets, such as a warrior's acute yet relaxed state of alert and *mushin,* which is Japanese for *empty mind (pure awareness without thought),* were all considered elements that could be intentionally learned, perfected, and automated. The wonderful thing about today's scientific research is that it is able to prove that this approach works and expand what can be done with this great attentional machinery in all areas of life.

YOU CAN TRAIN ALTERED MIND-SETS

If you want to begin your workday with a specific mind-set, such as a relaxed alertness, you can train it. Similarly, if you want to alter your mind-set for other points in the day, you can train that as well, and you can automatize it to click in at targeted work situations and goals.

As researchers note, today "the mainstream of psychology accepts both the fact of conscious or willed causation of mental and behavioral processes and the fact of automatic or environmentally triggered processes. The debate has shifted from the existence (or not) of these different causal forces to the circumstances under which one versus the other controls the mind. Is everyday life mainly comprised of consciously or nonconsciously caused evaluations, judgments, emotions, motivations, and behavior?"[6] The overwhelming conclusion is that *automind* rules most of your day. But still…it is possible to extend control over the important moments.

Consider this. One year, with colder weather just around the corner, I decided to change a bulb in our driveway lamppost. Not giving it much thought, and with my dog watching from below, I climbed the ladder. Then I automatically removed the two screws that hold the top of the lamp in place. Next, I began to lift off the lid. I fully expected to be reaching in and unscrewing the light bulb in the next few seconds. I was focused on that specific goal, and my actions were totally on autopilot. Suddenly my dog began barking really loudly. Her bark, which I recognized as the one she used to warn us of danger, zapped me out of my automatic mind and sparked my attention. Now I tried to locate what she was barking at. She continued until I came down the ladder. I stepped back from the lamppost. At first, I didn't see anything. Perhaps she was game playing. I climbed the ladder again. As I approached the lamp with focused curiosity, I could see a dark shadow sprawled across the bulb. Examining it further, I discovered it was a bat. Nothing up until that day could have predicted that for me. I was beyond surprised. My mind and body leaped into automatic mode. I literally jumped off the ladder. "Whoa!" I shouted. "Oh, wow." My next action, to figure out how to get the bat out of the lamp, was automatically and environmentally motivated. Since I didn't know what steps to take next, I simply got myself and the dog out of the way and left. For me, the best option to resolve the problem was to find out how to do it and then execute the likely solution. Consulting the good Dr. Google (which is what many of my associates are calling Google searches these days), I discovered several possibilities. The one that worked best was to just give the little creature some time on its own. I followed that advice, and when I returned I found that the bat—once left to itself—had flown away. Afterward, I knew that I shouldn't forget the lessons I'd learned anytime soon. There are plenty more places in our neck of the Berkshire woods where bats like to hang.

REMEMBER YOUR BRAIN'S LANGUAGE

In chapter 2 we discussed repetition as one of the brain's favorite languages. Amazingly we are not just capable of making automatizations out of will or unconsciously, but the process itself is an automatization. All you have to do is repeat something enough times, in relatively the same circumstance, and your brain—consciously or unconsciously—gets the message that this is how you want to act in that situation, and thus your behavior is automatized. This, as we said, can happen as an act of will or without your awareness. What Koch and Crick seemed to notice is that these zombie-like triggers can disappear from your awareness once formed (remember, that's the point), yet they continue to trigger as if out of nowhere so fast and stealthily you don't know it's happening. The key is that once you consciously identify a need for change and improvement, you'll have to shine a light on your zombies, since they control the majority of what you do and experience.

Consider the following story. Frank, a 26-year-old marketing specialist office worker who had been at his job for two years, wanted change at work. He didn't know exactly what change he wanted, but he felt that he was ready for something positive and new. Here's how it all played out.

One morning, Frank walked into work. From afar, he noticed his boss's abrupt body movement as the boss picked up some materials waiting in the reception area—a detail of particular interest to Frank's zombies. Frank instantly assumed his boss was in a negative mood, so he retreated to his own office and prepared to start his work for the day. He went through all his usual rituals before actually plunging in: laying out necessary paperwork on his desk, checking email, listening to voicemail messages, and drinking his coffee. He felt less focused than usual, and he worked slower than he had intended. He rationalized that this was because he hadn't gotten his full eight hours of Zs the night before. But there was more. Could it be that observing his boss's body language had slowed Frank's overall energy and focus? Yes, in a variety of ways. Let's see how.

By afternoon, Frank had gotten enough work done to satisfy the day's load. He felt lackluster about it, but that was not unusual. A little later, he droned over to an all-office conference his boss had arranged for that day. Frank felt unmotivated and detached throughout the meeting. Among the talking points, his boss offered up a new professional development project for any three employees who expressed interest. The boss explained that one of the area's universities, a nationally top-rated institution, was offering a summer institute to study creativity. He detailed that the institute consisted of creative thinking combined with creative and technical writing and would be awarding participants with writing certificates. "No hitches," the boss emphasized. "Want to do it? I anticipate several future projects and possibly two new employee positions for individuals who have these skills."

What happened next may surprise you, or perhaps you've made similar hasty decisions yourself. Under Frank's radar, expectation, predictability, various zombies, and unconscious goals determined the outcome for him. He passed on the opportunity without giving it much thought. Later, however, he used the technique of reflection to help remove the veil.

That night after dinner, Frank sat quietly in his living room.

He reflected upon his lack of motivation toward his boss's offer. He tried to trace the footprints of his decision in reverse. Why had he been so nonchalant about the opportunity? His trek led him to, among other things, images of his domineering father—his disappointment in Frank through most of his teen years and the tongue lashings whenever he felt that way. He wanted Frank to do what he wanted him to do, from which electives to take at school to whom to befriend to what major he would pursue in college. But most prominent in Frank's memory was his father's abrupt body language whenever he pontificated. That image, Frank began to see, was his father's brand, so to speak. Whenever Frank saw someone moving in a similar manor, it triggered a chain of negative vibes, unconscious zombies that unplugged his enthusiasm and aimed his goals in an opposite direction. Such an unconscious experience had just happened with his boss.

A few days later, Frank heard through the grapevine that three of his coworkers had taken the boss's offer to attend the institute. He mentally told himself off for making such a dumb decision. Determined to look into his conundrum further, Frank made a list of ways that an alternate decision may have suited him. He noted that he liked to write, he wanted a promotion sooner than later, he expected a vertical employment move to another institution in his future, and a tech writing certificate from a major university and a promotion could help get him there. Time-traveling forward into this visualized scenario, it looked like accepting his boss's offer could have served him well. But he had lost the opportunity.

A few weeks before the institute was to begin, one of Frank's colleagues had to cancel out. Since Frank had already done some good mind-work digging out an old zombie, he offered to take his colleague's place and got the seat.

Did Frank get rid of the automatized behavior engendered by a domineering person in his life? No, it would take more than one episode to do that. (We'll look at how you can weaken and remove these zombies in later pages.) However, Frank's reflection helped him trace an automatization that had been plaguing his goals for years, and he was able to dilute its influence over this current and important decision.

Some things turned out as Frank had strategized. He received the certificate, which later helped him acquire two promotions rather than one. No other work projects were ever developed, but when other employees were laid off, Frank was able to hold on to his position, which he attributed in part to his cooperation and better bonding with coworkers and his boss after participating in the institute. Looking back, he now sees that the big surprise came several years later, when he used a formula he'd learned at the institute to write a book on a topic that had nothing to do with the job that had paid to send him there. The book's success brought him much satisfaction and with it a whole new career.

Life can be full of nice surprises. When you learn how to identify potential zombies that are responsible for some of your decisions; how to consider their role in your motivation and ambitions; how to listen to your inner voice; and, ultimately, how to create a more self-aware, authentic reality for yourself, you will open the door to many positive experiences.

TRY THIS!

Consider a current career option that you may have dismissed— one that the little voice in your head keeps looping back into your awareness, a signal that you might like to rethink your position. Maybe it is an opportunity to cross-train with another department, to pursue a degree, or to travel. You may feel that pursuing the prospect is a pain just now, but take a moment to visualize ahead one year from now and then five years from now. Ask yourself questions like these: How would it look from there? What do I want to be doing then? Might the endeavor now help take the "dead end" sign off a position seemingly going nowhere? Might it provide new energy? Could it engage new social connection or personal fulfillment? This is all part of becoming more self-aware and using that awareness to create links to deeper, more satisfying work-related goals and a better life for you.

Look ahead 10 years. What do you see as a must-do-now from that vantage point? Is there anything you might do differently now as a result? Greater self-awareness will help you make better imminent decisions. Remember, it will also guide and strengthen your attentional beam to details that are useful in reaching your goals, and it will inhibit its attachment to those that are unrelated. By using your attention to harmonize your daily experience, imminent goals, and inner purpose, you will feel you are on a sweeter track.

YOUR MIND ON NEED

Need can drive you to excellence or it can mind-blind you. We are wired to be driven by needs and attach our focus to details that we believe will satisfy our needs. At the same time, needs cause us to inhibit details we perceive as unrelated to them— kind of like the concept of having a one-track mind. What's tricky is that just because we perceive something as unrelated to a need, that doesn't mean it truly is—especially when your focus is imminently need-driven.

Further, needs source from all sorts of places, including from your thoughts, beliefs, values, feelings (physical and emotional), memories, and the constant developing stream of internal and external details.

TRY THIS!

It may be fun to take a moment to consider an instance from today when you were suddenly sidetracked by an unexpected need. Ask yourself these questions:

What was the sudden need that I felt?

What were the interrupting thought(s) and/or feeling(s) that spurred the need?

What did I do next?

What was the basis for what I was thinking or feeling (e.g., a personal belief, an institutional value, my usual pattern)?

Is my action something I want to keep as a response or is it something I want to change?

Needs can hack your automatic functions and derail a goal you are pursuing in an instant. This is why, say, when you get hungry later in the evening, you head for your habitual, pre-set hunger crusher, whether it's something healthy like fruit or something unhealthy like fries or pizza. You just do it. Same when you're at work and you need to blow off steam, so you go to your usual stress buster, whether that's a coworker you have been using as a sounding board, a short break to walk it off, or a stream of bawdy pejoratives wailing in your head. You just do it. The essential question is this: *Should you?* Is the action in your best interest? Initially it may deliver relief for a few minutes, but how are you going to feel about it later that evening or the next day? Will it cramp your headspace or loosen it? How might it affect you a week or year from now? Widening your attentional lens, would you have done anything differently?

In our earlier example, Frank had an internal need and desire for change, but it was trumped by negative emotions stirred by his boss's body language, which was external and environmental. These details were psychologically connected to Frank's very old, hardwired, flight-or-fight survival mechanisms, and that was all it took for Frank to withdraw as soon as the offer to attend a summer institute came out of his boss's mouth. In the example, Frank's emotional need to withdraw inhibited his attention to any positive details he could have registered about a good opportunity. Don't get me wrong—Frank didn't have much choice, given his zombies. Reason is rarely ever a match for on-the-spot emotion, which is why reflection is such an essential key.

Lucky for Frank he later allowed his self-talk (inner voice) to enter his awareness. That opened up his subtler need for career advancement, which had been hacked earlier by his emotional zombies. Frank's reflection generated a deeper self-awareness. It helped him see what could have been a deeper goal, one that was more in alignment with authentic motivations. All of this finally led him to acquire a seat in the institute, upon availability. If the spot had not opened up, Frank likely would have found other ways to pursue his newly identified goals.

Frank's path is no panacea or instant cure-all, but awareness is a significant first step toward self-regulation. His inner talk tipped him off that something was wrong with his decision. His willingness to follow this possibility to the next step was crucial. In fact, willfulness is one of your takeaway points in order to identify and regulate your own automatizations.

In your academic or work ventures you have probably encountered some version of the popular *idiot test*, which is supposed to help people learn to read directions thoroughly. The test instructs readers to follow a set of numbered directions. The first directive always says something like, "Read everything before doing anything." The operative words are *read before doing.* The majority of people, however, just barrel ahead and attend to the directives, only to discover that the last one says "Ignore all previous directions" or "Do only steps 1 and 2." Most people—aimed at fulfilling their need to check off one directive after another and to get the job done ASAP—default to their usual way of sailing through directions, failing to read through all of them first and doing a lot of unnecessary work.

The test is meant to teach us a lesson about following directions. It usually works. Old dysfunctional zombies weaken and extinguish. Afterward, no matter if it's an idiot test or an important contract, you tend to read through the material first.

Automatic hacks appear in more places than you might expect. Just thinking about doing something, for instance, increases your likeliness of doing it, whether you're thinking about a desire to tell someone off or about taking any other negative or positive action. Further, once you make a steady diet of thinking a certain way, it will become automatic without your consent and can trigger behaviors to your detriment. The good news is that it is possible to regulate this robotic behavior.

YOUR ATTENTION'S CEO

This is where self-awareness teams with your *executive attention*, the top of your attention's chain of command. As we indicated in the introduction, evolution has gifted every healthy brain (which most of us enjoy) with a kind of command control. This capacity is all about choice—the ability to select one detail or daily path over another. It is your focus's CEO. Your executive attention has split-second capability to overrule even strong impulses and attractions for more favorable—even understated—options.

Importantly, this mechanism can regulate your automatizations so that they better support your daily goals. You can choose, for instance, to hold off on something you think you need at the moment for something you can predict is better down the line. An example might be that you forego applying with an organization you've always wanted because you know you will have an MBA or PhD in hand by the end of the year. In this way, we are all wired with the ability to identify and prioritize moments in our lives. Executive attention is what takes over when a parent hustling to strap three screaming children into car seats before loading groceries into the car notices in a flash that one of the children has unstrapped and is heading into traffic. It's the employee who, on a Friday afternoon, avoids letting fly a mouthful of emotionally charged language about a supervisor, opting instead to go home at the end of the day feeling lighter and more secure.

As you advance into adulthood, your executive attention matures and is visible in your ability to resolve conflicts, correct errors, and plan new actions. It is a necessary mechanism in situations in which automatized behaviors are inadequate—anything from how you interpret a coworker's body language to how you deal with an unexpected problem at work. Essential for most life skills, your executive attention can regulate a range of networks, including emotional responses, sensory data, memory, and—as we have discussed—automatizations. This allows you to extinguish, edit, and/or replace robotic circuits with ones that are more advantageous to your daily workplace goals. Like Frank's decision to rethink his feelings about attending the institute, your executive attention can target appropriate internal and external information and lead you to more satisfying conclusions.

Identify and renovate harmful zombies.

CHAPTER EXERCISES

Using the Restaurant Test

This activity helps you identify internal and external details that trigger automatizations. Next time you are in a restaurant or a café, scan the room. Pick one individual you feel a positive attraction to and another you feel negative about. Be sure to choose from people you do not know. Then trace your mental and emotional footprints. Ask yourself to identify what exactly is influencing your feelings: a face or facial expression, a voice, something said, a thought, an article, body language, a detail in memory? Ask yourself, "Are any of these influencers reasonable upon reconsideration? If not, why?"

Controlling Your Zombies

Use executive attention. Pick one workplace skill you want to improve that will give you some real mileage on a current goal you are pursuing. For example, let's say that you feel you have developed a tendency to cut off coworkers or clients before they finish what they are saying, or that you have been fading out when they speak. (Both issues would cause you to miss important data and/or mess up your relationship.) Sketch a strategy that includes mindful self-awareness, mindful reflection, and mindful attention. To practice self-awareness, consider why you wish to control the situation. Ask, "How do I want to present myself? How have I presented myself in the past? Do I want to do anything differently? Why is it important for me to control this situation now? How can it affect future goals?"

Reflect on applying your strategy in a typical workday situation. Prompts that serve as triggers can help. Create a mantra to condition the behavior you want to control, such as, "Listen more than you talk" or "Be in listen mode." Then apply it on the fly, in real time.

Remember, you can automatize these skills just by making them a regular pattern. Take a moment later in your day, after you have tried your strategy, to reflect on how the situation played out. This will give you the opportunity to edit and fine-tune your strategy and to update the automatization you are creating. In the future, it will help you perform the way you desire more consistently and in line with your perceived goals.

4

Squashing Information

Rule #4

*Use your brain's capacity to identify and squash
details that are disconnected to your goals.*

If you want high-quality attention, you can't—that's right, *can't*—
pay attention to everything that comes at you. So, as we've
discussed, nature has endowed our brain with a *squashing
mechanism* to additionally help us filter information. It will
become clearer and clearer throughout this book that when
your mechanisms for filtering through details are weak or fail,
you are most vulnerable to distraction, stress, fatigue, overload,
error, and dissatisfaction. You have that discombobulated feeling when your mind seems to bottleneck on overload and you
just can't see your way. On the other hand, practicing each of the
12 rules will sweeten those mechanisms so they'll hum for you.

Squashing is a term I will use to give you the mental image of
clearing data, putting it out of sight and out of mind. The goal is
to free up space in your mind and prevent data overload. Think
of external and internal details. Externally, you can squash the

invasion of irrelevant environmental details, such as machine noise in your workspace, chatter, the road crew working outside your window, or the scent of donuts calling to you from the break room. Internally, you can knock out influences such as derailing thoughts, memories, emotions, and images of past behaviors and experiences. Any of these distracters can rapidly drive your focus off target, so you want to deal with them.

You've no doubt experienced getting sideswiped by uninvited, nerve-racking details that have prevented you from flowing through a task: a colleague harping on about your contribution to a project, a supervisor making unreasonable demands, an impossible deadline to meet, a growing list of unanswered emails, and so forth. Not only can they disrupt you, they can also trigger negative behaviors. If you don't control them, you'll usually get overwhelmed, further spiking feelings of stress and conflict, and your ability to exercise control over personal negative behavior patterns will weaken.

At times like this, we all tend to dip into a regimen of worsening responses, just when we most need to rein in what's out of control. It's a nasty cycle. What's more, since your attention's CEO is now too stressed to take command, these are the times your bad zombies—remember them?—like to dig in deeper to keep you on autopilot, leaving you with little choice in balancing your behavior and thinking. The high stress fuels your worst coping skills, and as a result, the tasks and your already degenerating responses spiral downhill fast. Your mind is now fertile for your favorite knee-jerk reactions and habitual blunders. This is also the crossroad where your task-related judgments and responses seem to degenerate as your brain gets involved in why things went wrong.[1] So, on top of it all, you are now acting in an obsessively compulsive way.

One way to squash this kind of negative loop is to check it at the door, so to speak. Don't stay in that loop, repeating the same goal-hacking, judgment-bulldozing behavior yet again. Instead, take a short break to recharge your energies. The less mental energy you have, the more difficult it will be to regain balance. Remember, good focus requires energy, so it's important to stop imploding. Just lock the zombie in the proverbial box and tell yourself you are leaving it behind. Research shows that time off to reboot will do you more good than continuing in a negative behavioral loop or slowing down in an attempt to get a grip on the situation.[2]

The reward for learning how to squash focus stealers is that you can get rid of things that could block your present moment *before* they drive you off target. So, start by keeping your action choices open, giving clearer consideration to what you need moment by moment—and most importantly, keeping your Zen.

In the coming pages, we will look at several other ways to use your brain's attention machinery to zero in among the bombardment of details going through your head while on task. I will also show you how to better squash irrelevancies while keeping your focus and capturing what's important.

CHECK IN WITH HEADQUARTERS

Earlier, we discussed self-awareness as your hub for attentional regulation—your headquarters, so to speak. So the next way to squash information is by making yourself preaware. This begins with checking into headquarters to acquire an understanding of your previous behavioral patterns when you are in pursuit of a specific goal. Such understanding helps organize your approach by highlighting which prior patterns worked and which didn't, which to encourage again or which to disengage. For instance, was your pattern to represent yourself as aggressive or calm in a certain situation? Light or serious? Flexible or set? What's your best representation now? The effort to self-examine is worth it, and it's easy.

Let's say that any time an employee communicates with a certain tone, your pattern is to become overly aggressive. Making yourself preaware of this behavioral pattern gives you the option of trying to disengage the aggressive behavior before it triggers in real time when you next communicate with an employee who uses that tone. Self-awareness enables you to choose the more situationally advantageous behavior—in this case, engendering a quieter, more relaxed encounter.

SQUASH IRRELEVANT SETTINGS AND CHANGE YOUR RESULTS

Stacey is employed by an urban medical center. She is one of three individuals who schedule patient referrals as well as follow-ups. Her preferred MO is presenting herself as upbeat and relaxed whether on the phone or in the office. But she knows that when she is bothered by something, whether it is an incident at work or from her private life, it can do a number on her friendly profile. When feelings intrude, she actually feels herself slow down in a detrimental sense, as if she has been unplugged. Her movements, concentration, memory, and mood all fatigue. She has come to realize that this mind-set leads to disorganization as well as miscommunication with patients and coworkers. She knows it leaves her prone to billing mistakes and other paperwork errors. Conversely, she has received many compliments from patients on how her hospitable, more amiable demeanor comforts them during their hard times. She is aware that these moments build her positive energy for daily challenges.

Stacey was recently responsible for a series of form errors

regarding patient insurance coverage. These incited her to reflect on the situation. When she played the crucial scenes in her head like a movie, she saw a pattern.

Tracing her footprints in one error, she discovered she'd been ruminating over the fact that a new supervisor was set to take over the management of office affairs the following week. Not only did this split her focus as she went from completing one piece of work to another, it also consumed her positivity with thoughts like these: *I just went out to lunch with my current supervisor. I thought our relationship was open. Why didn't she tell me she was leaving? How will I get along with the new person? Is my job still safe?* Then her mind leaped to her personal finances—which depended on her employment. A river of stress fogged her head all day as she spoke with patients, filling out their forms and schedules. Her energy dipped and her mental acuity fatigued. Upon reflection, she could see that her mind wasn't where she needed it to be.

Reflection works. It helps sort out why and how we slip up on occasion. It also helps us locate where our mind needs to be to avoid error and thus tells us what influencers to squash. Leading to self-awareness, reflection is a solid step toward solutions, for Stacey and the rest of us who practice it.

Digging deeper, Stacy saw there had been more gnawing at her. The next focus invader she identified was a situation from home accessing her mind at work. It involved a circumstance between her son and his best friend, who had suddenly begun to turn on him at school. As with most parents, just because she was at work didn't mean her parental problem stayed home. Instead, it was living in her head as she tried to focus on patients.

As we've seen, self-awareness through reflection helps expose specific details that pop up and hack our ability to navigate daily tasks fluidly. The good news is that with understanding come compassion for ourselves and more civility for others.

You are human; breathe easy. We are all susceptible to attention stealers like these. However, knowing that is not enough. What you do next is very important.

YOU CAN OPEN OR CLOSE THE GATE

You are your attentional gatekeeper. This gives you the power to activate certain details, letting them into your focus with more capture, and to inhibit other details squashing them out.

During the 1960s, scientists enjoyed likening the mind to a computer. Since then, the computer analogy has been replaced with the image of several computers. Each controls various areas of the brain, including language, motor skills, pain, pleasure, and emotions. You can imagine each as a separate computer with specific data to its particular area. Each computer reports to your attention's CEO, your executive attention. As top dog in your attention's chain of command, it has the power to *gate* what information is relevant and engage it and to gate what information is not relevant and disengage that. Not only can you use your executive attention to decide what you want to respond to, but you can also use it to determine how, when, and why you will respond to it, as well as to override other stronger urges fighting for your attention in any given moment.

Back to Stacey's work situation, by selecting to turn off urges to ruminate about her supervisor and son at work, she could make a world of difference in her outcome. In other words, consciously selecting what details to squash will be Stacey's (and our) next step in the process of separating useful details from distracters. This involves another attentional engine: your selective attention (as discussed in chapter 1). When you use the option to toggle your spotlight back and forth among incoming data and select what detail you'd like in your head and which you'd rather inhibit, you can preset your mind to turn off the dysfunctional thoughts, feelings, and negative zombie patterns you are trying to control. In fact, the process itself begins squashing irrelevancies. When they pop up in real time, you automatically pay less attention to them. Science has long known that keeping your goal/task clear in your mind at this stage also greases this machinery. So it also works as a preset to strengthen the inhibition of non-goal-related details as well as to promote focus on relevant details.

We are droning around 96 percent of the day or so, yes, but if we can improve on that percentage just a little—just for the important moments, even—then the remaining 4 percent or so becomes significant to painting our own unique canvas of life. Importantly, these can add up to formidable successes. It is in these moments that we exercise our will and become who we want to be.

We are all momentarily attentionally deficient in some way, particularly as we move from one daily task to another. There are just too many details wanting to get into our skull. Think of an Olympic skier making split-second adjustments to stay on course on her way down a mountain or the tennis pro making superhuman shots look easy by selecting *to close the gate to* dysfunctional, momentarily irrelevant details. This works for you, too. Just identifying a thought or concern and telling yourself, "This is not for now," will psychologically and biologically get the process going.

Reflection plays in once again, providing you with the preknowledge and self-awareness to better understand why certain details are relevant, how much they are relevant, and where in real life your goal will require more focus. While making it possible to squash dysfunctional details and other distracters, the combination of reflection, preawareness, and understanding will help you keep the gate open to advantageous details and better catch them in real time.

TRY THIS!

It's essential to know your distracters. Visualization will help expose habitual behavior patterns that are not working in your favor. You can use visualization to start squashing task-irrelevant details that are driving you off course. Your job is to take a closer look at what's going on in your mind and what you can do instead. Let's begin.

1. Pick a work task that you have usually performed well but have recently begun to mess up.
2. Imagine yourself in the task. Play it in your head. Go over the crucial scenes slowly. Try to identify what thoughts, feelings, or details are pulling your attention away from the task.
3. Next, visualize going through the work scenario again, eliminating the invading influencers. See yourself using alternate functional behaviors in their place. As an example, if you are ruminating on what your new supervisor may be like, see yourself squashing the tendency at first sight and telling yourself that now is not the time. Offer yourself an alternative, like, "I will think it through in a calming manner after work as I treat myself to a relaxing massage." Then see yourself diving back into the flow of your work.

CUES

Using self-reflection, an engineer named Alex realized that whenever he got a workplace issue in his head, he wanted it resolved immediately. This usually involved discussing it with his supervisor, so it was his habit to jet to her office by the end of the day and lay it out. Organizational protocol required appointments except in urgent cases, but Alex usually ignored that. However, upon reflection, he realized that when he did just drop in, his timing was frequently off. His boss would be on a call or in a scheduled appointment with someone else. He'd often find himself having to wait for her, which was frustrating to him and put some speed bumps in his finesse. Turned out she wasn't as disposed to receiving him in those instances, either. It also dawned on him that frequently when he'd give the issue a few more days, things often took care of themselves. He realized that he needed to alter his automatic approach.

One way to squash dysfunctional urges is by creating a cue designed to turn them off. Our minds love mental cues. We use them to make healthy food choices, get to bed early, and make important telephone calls on time. To make cues highly effective, situationally powerful, and ultimately automatized, however, we need to practice them until they become ingrained.

All kinds of cues are available. One of my favorite types is *word cues,* which I call power words. As an example, to help athletes sharpen performance skills, word cues can be tailored to a particular game, opponent, or specific point in athletic performance, such as when a runner nears the finish line and tells herself, "Pour it on!" Similarly, beginning martial artists may prompt themselves with a cue like, "Put your hip into it." The International Tennis Federation, as another example, recommends phrases with an instructional component, like "Watch the ball, take the ball early, follow-through," or motivational or emotional words like "Relax, positive, strong, move."[3] The key to creating word cues is to use short and simple language that will engage the desired action.

Some quick-acting workplace word cues that you might like to put in your pocket are these:

No more than five minutes.
Repeat aloud.
Quit multitasking.
Be proactive.
Enter with positivity.
Leave with positivity.
Consider the other person's perspective.
Widen your spotlight.

Importantly cues are more than just reminders; they have the same activation and inhibition power as visualization and reflection. It's most effective to create your own cues for specific situations you want to improve. You won't need many, and it's better not to overwhelm yourself. Picking one or two essential situations and one or two cues that will give you the most success is a good way to start.

Returning to Alex's story, he decided to create a cue to resist his urge to approach his boss for immediate closure. After considering various options, he chose to use a musical cue to add more oomph to his intention. He discovered that making a playlist of upbeat songs with self-empowering lyrics did the trick. The playlist's quick tempos and lyrics gave him the energy to resist his urges. He used his playlist randomly as the weekend approached and especially as he started to feel he needed to talk to his boss. It was as easy as pushing the play button.

REINFORCING WITH A SCAN

Alex doubled up his ability to squash his tendency to carelessly pop in on his boss for things he didn't really need help with or would later regret pursuing. To further resist his urges and replace them with subtler, more effective choices, he used a self-scan. Here's how it worked.

Before his urges became overwhelming, he paused to ask himself questions like these:

Why do I feel it is necessary to speak to my boss?

How did my drop-in approach work in the past when circumstances were similar?

How would this time be different?

What would my boss prefer me to do, given my concerns (See her by appointment? Figure things out myself?)

If I stop in to see her, how will my action affect or contribute to my current job?

How will it help me build toward employment beyond this one?

Remember, good attention is controlled attention guided by good choices. For Alex, using musical cues reinforced with a self-scan helped him squash ineffective behaviors down the line and broadened his options for better choices. Eventually, the motivational energy he sought to strengthen his choices became automatic, and he no longer required the cues.

TOP-DOWN IN A BOTTOM-UP WORK WORLD

The free flow of details that builds upon itself into personal events or experiences is known as *bottom-up processing*. For example, when you examine a spreadsheet of purchases to locate any waste in spending and then several culprits suddenly appear to you, you are relying mostly on bottom-up processing.

The opposite is top-down processing. Top-down processing uses a cue of sorts in that you already know what you are looking for. For example, when you are looking at a calendar to schedule a trip that does not conflict with any potential holidays, you are relying on top-down information—the holidays you already know are listed on the calendar. Telling your friend that he'll find you at the Goth concert because you'll be wearing a yellow T-shirt is also a top-down cue. A top-down prompt helps squash irrelevant information in your way and makes your target stand out significantly more.

The two worlds of bottom-up and top-down and are closely related. Ever have the feeling of knowing what you're looking for, but you just haven't found it yet? When you feel this way you are often relying on both top-down and bottom up processing. Paul McCartney's songwriting style, for instance, demonstrates how both of these types of processing can work together to achieve a goal. McCartney's poet friend Allen Ginsberg encouraged Paul to use a "First thought, best thought" bottom-up strategy when it came to writing, and McCartney has added his own idea on the strategy: "It doesn't always work," he said, "but as a general idea I will try and do that and sometimes I come out with a puzzling set of words that I have no idea what I mean, and yet I've got to kind of make sense of it and follow the trail."[4] Talking about writing his iconic song "Eleanor Rigby," McCartney mentioned that as he was composing it, he was missing the name for the character in the lyrics. As a top-down cue, he was aware the name would have to fit the music. In particular, the name would need to fit the rhythm. So he had a sense of what he was looking for—but he wouldn't know what his solution was until he saw it. It would have to emerge from bottom-up. McCartney recalled he was in Bristol during that time period and saw the name of a shop called Rigby's. He tied that to the name of a woman he was working with on *Help!* whose name was Eleanor. And voila! Eleanor

Rigby emerged—a perfect fit for his song. Then sometime later, he needed a name for the vicar character in the same tune. He got out the phone book, flipped through the Macs (because, as he recalled, he and Lennon wanted it to be Mac something, again a top-down cue) until he got to Mackenzie. Suddenly there it was, and the character, Father McKenzie, was born.[5]

McCartney's story is a reminder of how top-down processing can heighten your ability to zero in on important, goal-related details emerging from everyday bottom-up experiences. Yes, this approach can put restrictions and boundaries on experiences as they emerge, but I urge you not to stop at that thought. Somewhat counterintuitively, fresh insights, vibrant new connections, and organizational patterns will still emerge when the these two forms of processing team. Try pairing them to get a jump ahead in your daily pursuits.

CHANGE WITH CHANGE

Fluid flexibility is important in all forms of goal pursuit. The idea is to go with the flow, so to speak, and adapt—identifying which incoming details must be squashed to stay on course and which must be activated. The answer will grow out of the situation. And because things can change at any moment, keeping a fluid focus is important.

To achieve this kind of fluidity, you must keep a wide spotlight on emerging environmental and internal details enhanced with cue awareness. This strategy supports the processing of continuous up-to-the minute updates. It automatically links you to previous behaviors in similar experiences plus updates and coordinates them with your present goal. This ensures that you are well updated in regard to your next series of task-related behaviors.

Once you are aware of your cues and place yourself into a goal-driven experience—whether through reflection, visualization, or in real time—flexibility within your squashing system kicks in naturally and adjusts as you work into your task. Additionally, the use of cues (all your presets) and goal reminders help make your attention stronger and further squash distracters. This is important so I will emphasize it again: using cues and goal reminders will keep you on course, with higher energy, better attentional inhibition and activation, and greater capture of important details. Such tiny adjustments can make a big difference in results. They will synchromatically help you destress and prevent conflicts of thought, feelings, and behavior so that you will keep your mind (and performance) flowing. When these systems are in place, you feel and appear more on top of your game, confident, and proficient. "Being flexible when it comes to work is worth a lot. Employees who approach their job with a flexible mind-set are typically more highly valued by employers."[6] I call getting all these components working together toward your goal *synchrony*. Managers appreciate flexibility in employees, and employees appreciate flexibility in managers.[7] Flexibility is a win-win all around.

FLEXIBILITY IS A TWO-WAY SCENE

What's Bad May Sometimes Be Good

You've probably noticed that hardly anything in attention training is always one-sided, so flexibility is key. Although we have been discussing ways to squash irrelevant information from our attention, there are also times you will want to open the gate to invite distracters to ensure that you don't miss something important. There is a traditional saying in holistic arts, "Keep one eye on the target and the other on the way." Some of the significant discoveries that were nudged by distractions that someone paid attention to include DNA, penicillin, the microwave, and Velcro; all were born out of details that could have otherwise just been dismissed as a distraction had their discoverers not opened the gate and given them some attention.[8]

The film *Christmas in the Air*, with Catherine Bell, is a light-hearted example of how both top-down and bottom-up processing achieve some great results once you add some flexibility. In the film, Bell's character, Lydia, is a professional organizer who is attracted to a young widower named Robert, who has a young son. Robert is Lydia's disorganized opposite. In the end, both characters grow when they open up to the other's world. Robert successfully crushes his goal of presenting a new toy line to a superstore and deepens his bond with his son; Lydia finds that her top-down insistence on organization has cut off some of the sweeter rewards that just letting things emerge can sometimes fuel. In the end, flexibility and synchrony rule. The characters and audience clearly learn that there are two sides to organized focus and disorganization. As the marketing copy explains, "While she is intent on helping him straighten out details he had long ignored, Robert teaches the buttoned-up Lydia that messiness can be a delightful part of life."[9]

FOCUS/EXECUTE, CLEAR/REPEAT

At this point, you are familiar with a set of tools presented in chapters 1 through 4 that will strengthen your power of focus. These include boosting mindfulness, awareness, and your ability to capture important detail in an information stream by using a variety of techniques, including

- Repetition
- Self-awareness
- Visualization
- Reflection
- Cues
- Inhibition and activation
- Self-scans

Although you must learn these skills individually, with practice they begin melding into a new way of thinking and attending to important (and even unimportant) things in your workday. Consequently, I want to end this chapter with a formula you can use to train your mind to finally zero in, execute your best action, cool off, and keep flowing toward whatever comes next.

Here is the formula: *focus/execute/rinse/repeat*. Think of it as a cue. It will help you bring all the pieces together as you adjust your lens from wide to narrow. Whenever you have an invading thought, use *mushin* (empty mind) to let it float on by like a reflection on water, squashing irrelevancies out of sight and out of mind effortlessly. Or you may choose to follow them—also effortlessly—to see where they may lead. With practice, this procedure and all the other mechanics you are incorporating into it will become automatic and keep you flowing.

 Use your brain's capacity to identify and squash detail that is disconnected to your goals. Train the mind to zero in, execute your best action, cool off, and keep flowing. Then go on to your next goal.

CHAPTER EXERCISES

Each of these techniques will help you talk to your brain and begin to regulate the way you are paying attention.

Using a Power Word

Pick one upcoming situation you'd like to have better control over. Visualize yourself in that situation and some of the behaviors that you have employed in the past. Remind yourself what your overall goal is. Ask yourself, "Why is this goal important? What other personal goals might my performance in this situation relate to?" Pick the most important behavior you need to ensure that you perform well. Ask yourself, "What elements of this behavior do I want to keep? What elements do I want to edit?" Create a top-down cue that can keep you focused on that detail, such as "Enter with positivity; leave with positivity," or "Not now; wait a day or two."

Using a Musical Cue

Music permeates every part of the brain in milliseconds. We used the word *computers* to refer to these various brain parts earlier in this chapter. Accordingly, music can imbed new habits (behavioral patterns you have associated with the music) deep into the memory of each "computer" and serve as a great cue to prompt specific actions in specific situations. Follow the directions for the first exercise, but instead of using a power word, find a song that you love and that energizes you toward one important aspect of hitting your goal. Use a line from the song that is special to you and your goal as your musical cue.

Using a Self-Scan

Often you can inhibit and/or activate things you know are going to come up in a forthcoming goal. Remember, in real time inhibited details will be impeded whereas activated details will be encouraged to engage. I recommend using this scan in advance of actual events to help sharpen your awareness before starting out. It can sharpen your clarity, improve your organization, heighten your attention in real time, and keep your focus on track.

To begin, mindfully ask yourself these questions:

- What is my present task?
- What external detail (environment, paperwork, materials, competing tasks, coworkers) is goal-related and something I should pay attention to?

Acknowledge any external detail vying for your attention that is not related to your goal. Do a reality check on it. For example, the need to take a break to take a medication at a specific time would be real and acceptable, but the need to recreationally check your Facebook account for information that is not task-related would not. If it's an unacceptable interference, visualize yourself disengaging from it and determine the appropriate time to do so. This approach primes your inhibition to squash that behavior.

Next, ask yourself these questions.

- What internal detail is popping up as you visualize approaching your task that appears supportive? What makes it supportive? For example, you may feel excitement about your activity because it will show personal attributes you've been dying to share and it will have legs toward extending you further with your employer. What internal detail is popping up that is interfering with your task? For example, you may feel your task is "beneath" you. What harm can this feeling present? For example, it might drive you to a disagreeable attitude and sarcastic language with your colleagues. If you discover an influencer that impedes your performance, consider the tools we have discussed in this chapter and pick one that will help you disengage it. Visualize yourself in the expected scenario disengaging any negative influencers.
- Visualize yourself engaged in the expected event, deactivating any negative influencers and activation positive influencers that will drive you to successfully hit your goal.

When opportunities present themselves in the real-time event, your mind will attend to them advantageously.

5

Size Doesn't Always Matter

Rule #5

*Learn from the big and small
(yet amazing) brains in nature.*

Today there is growing interest in studying brains of nonhuman animals. Such studies may seem counterintuitive, yet they are painting an amazing profile of the creatures we share the world with. Importantly, they help shape our understanding of our own mental capabilities. They offer alternative answers to problems we encounter in our attention, help us discover novel use of familiar attention tools, and allow us to identify tools unique to our own mind.

Explorations into the land of tiny creatures as well as larger animals have had a rich, rewarding history. In the 1940s, scientists discovered that bacteria had sex lives: "Microscopes proved the existence of single-celled bacteria. However, there was debate about whether bacteria had genes and what attributes they may have in common with higher life forms."[1] Researchers discovered that "during the process of conjugation, genes are exchanged through a mating channel that links two bacteria," settling the debate and proving bacteria actually do have sex. This research presented irrefutable support that genes are made of DNA.[2] This early research made it possible for scientists to advance into what was later to become genetic engineering and on to what we now know as genomics, which includes identification of an organism's complete set of DNA. In fact science has demonstrated that each genome has all of the information required to create and maintain an organism. In humans, a replica of the complete genome—more than 3 billion DNA base pairs, which look like rungs on a spiraling staircase in the double helix structure—appears in all cells that have a nucleus.[3]

Historically the Human Genome Project was an international research effort coordinated by the National Institutes of Health and the US Department of Energy, which set out to discover the sequence of the human genome and identify the genes it includes. The project formally started in 1990 and was so promising it finished in 2003, two years ahead of schedule. It has opened the doors for researchers to begin to comprehend the blueprint for human construction.[4] The research has panned out big-time. For instance, "In clinical medicine, the human genome gives important clues in the understanding of human diseases in terms of human biology and pathology. Medicine will be revolutionized in improving diagnosis, prognostic, treatments and prevention."[5]

Following a similar path, today scientists are tracing the footprints of consciousness in brains. This research is reminiscent of the frontier work on DNA. Although there are nearly a hundred billion neurons in the soft damp tissues of the brain, researchers aspire to one day map all the dots (neurons), so to speak, and do for neurologists, biologists, and psychologists what the human genome project has been doing for clinical medicine. Consciousness research has kept attention research even more in the limelight because the two networks, though different, are so closely related and in many cases dependent upon each other. The quickest way to self-improvement, greater mindfulness, peak performance, and happiness is via an evolved consciousness, and one of the greatest assets in doing *that* is developing better attention skills. So, yes, these systems are different, but for those of us interested in self-transformation, they do go hand in hand in interesting ways. A brief peek into how these mechanisms work together in nonhuman creatures can give us a clue as to the evolution of attention in us and inspire new answers to achieving sharper focus.

One thing we have learned from the continuous study of nonhuman subjects is that large-brained creatures, who can pay attention somewhat as we do, are not the sole owners of attention skills. Some brains are a quarter the size of a pinhead and others are even smaller, yet they are still paying attention. And we can learn from them both, big or small. For instance, ever try to catch a fruit fly, which has 100,000 neurons compared to our 100 billion? Yet so often a tiny insect like a fruit fly can outmaneuver us. On the other hand, they can't so easily outfox each other. The more evidence we mount on their navigation skills, the more reason to notice and wonder what ramifications this understanding might have for us. Nature is full of similar examples in brains other than human.

WHAT WE CAN LEARN FROM INSECT BRAINS

Humans are not the only animals wired with attention machinery. Other animals, including insects, must select from the barrage of details that vie for their attention in order to pilot their environments. It is well documented that this machinery provides them the ability to, among other things, protect against predators, locate good food sources, and find mates. Likely gifted by evolution, these features can achieve, even in small creatures, some functions similar to what we as well as other primates experience.[6]

Recall the famous mantra coined by boxing legend Muhammad Ali: *Float like a butterfly, sting like a bee—his hands can't hit what his eyes can't see.*[7] Could the famous mantra have served as a power word, a top-down cue for Ali? Could its imagery have inspired or guided movement that made him evasive to opponents yet capable of tagging them at will? Of course no one knows for sure, but quite likely all of that played in. You can learn to use similar psychological imagery to launch actions you want to hone. As we discussed in the last chapter, the sports world loves power words and phrases, especially ones that give us the "picture." But could there be even more to Ali's mantra? Why were early martial arts, for instance, based on the movements of large as well as tiny creatures? In fact, many styles of Kung Fu were created this way. Tiger, Cane, Eagle, and Mantis Kung Fu are just some of the styles.

Many of us have pictures and posters we look at that spark a certain mind-set when we want it. Sometimes we go to certain places that provide live images. We can even lie back and recall these and feel a good amount of that original spark.

We know now that images are energy and you can use them to alter your feelings and thoughts and even your motor skills— again, just think of the Ali mantra, *Float like a butterfly, sting like a bee...*

Energy is made up of two things: information and power. I call it *informed-power.* Not only is imagery one of the brain's favorite languages, but also the energy of imagery affects your brain's electrochemical activity, which generates your behavioral patterns. These patterns alter your mind-states and activate your motor skills, feelings, and thoughts. As we have mentioned previously, all you have to do is look at something or picture it in your mind and it can trigger a change in you. Once you do this repeatedly, such images and behaviors will become ingrained. With practice, they will activate automatically, and so will the effects they trigger. The Ali mantra was more than just poetry. It was good medicine. And you can create your own to enhance your focus and actions.

WHAT INSECT BRAINS CAN SHOW US ABOUT NEGOTIATING ENVIRONMENTS

Insect brains allow them to selectively negotiate their environments, a skill humans also need to efficiently and contentedly stay in flow. For example, "dragonflies have a sophisticated form of selective attention and can keep track of their prey while flying through swarms of other dragonflies."[8] Spending so much of my life in the Berkshire Mountains, I have watched dragonflies with absolute amazement as they land like tiny aircraft on a sun-warmed railing and wait until a mosquito or gnat (which most of us would have a difficult time catching) crosses their path. In a split second, the dragonfly will swoop in, catch its prey, and devour it, returning to its landing strip in the sun as relaxed as could be. Its focus/execute/rinse/repeat pattern is stunning. The movement from one step of the pattern to the next is so fast, smooth, and precise it would make any amateur athlete jealous. As soon as a certain threshold trips in its brain the dragonfly automatically goes into action.

TRY THIS!

We can learn to automatize our own attention by establishing thresholds we can set through our own mental wiring. This skill can have many creative applications; however, for this exercise let's explore creating a threshold to keep your mind flowing when you encounter everyday environmental distractions, such as a loud training session or deliveries that are taking place in the lobby outside your office or the overexcited colleagues in debate in the office next door. The fix can be as simple as setting up, in advance, an escape threshold to an alternate location, for when such interrupters occur. Decide on your threshold. Tell yourself that as soon as the distraction reaches a certain level, you will congenially relocate to a space you have already picked out and know will be comfortable, such as the outdoor picnic area when the weather is nice. If you cannot temporarily leave the workplace, perhaps there is another comfortable space within your organization where you can proceed without disturbance—an alternate office, meeting room, café, or comfy lobby. The idea is to have two plans, one to do your work in its usual space and the other set to a threshold that once reached you can quickly and smoothly and amiably slip into. This way you can act confidently and decisively keep your mind flowing and the quality of your work prime.

LEARN TO RESPOND AT THE
SPEED OF SOUND

As with humans, insects also rely on sound, including frequency, and they use auditory cues as top-down triggers to help them focus. Using separate streams of sound based on their frequency differences is called *auditory stream segregation*.[9] Crickets and bush crickets, for example, can distinguish between others in their species (lower frequency) and predators like bats (higher frequency). This discrimination is not dissimilar to that seen in vertebrates.[10] Bush crickets can zero in on sounds that they translate as "trouble ahead." These warn that a predator is nearby. Crickets will select to give that sound precedence even over sounds they may like better, such as a mating song beckoning from the distance. This kind of selective-like attention keeps them safe. In humans, this type of network links to states of self-movement, environment, and memory. [11]

As we've discussed, human brains love and use sound cues. And we can learn from small creatures to consider placing more emphasis on sound, especially in particular circumstances. Have you ever been hiking with someone who pushes a tree branch out of the way as you are following from behind? By the time you see the branch, it is usually too late. You can distinguish the sound of a swishing branch, however, quicker than you can see it, so you can get out of the way before it swipes you. Same with traffic sounds as you are driving—the sound of a screeching horn, siren, or brakes conveys a message even if you can't see the other vehicle. Same with malfunctioning machinery or alarms. Some workplace sounds are hazardous and provide us with quick, effective warnings. We also benefit from processing telltale sounds, like a client's foot-tapping anxiety or another's sigh of fatigue. And don't forget about positive sound cues: the excitement of a colleague's voice as he listens to you map out a creative idea or your supervisor's delight when she praises your work. These are all worth paying attention to and linking to your memory base. Sound bypasses your thinking brain and launches you right into action. When you start using sound to guide and train your responses, response time shortens and is more fluid and—if you've trained to act to specific sound—more accurate.

TRY THIS!

You can use sound to increase or calm mental and physical energy that wreaks havoc on your focus. This helps you meet tasks with more balanced energy so that you can ace them. Take a moment now to breathe in through your nose deeply and out through your mouth. Do this a few times. As you exhale through your mouth, listen to the "shhh" sound of your breath. Put your focus right on the sound. If you practice this very basic technique before and after moments of concentrated focus, you can use the actual sound to help reduce stressors that fatigue you. The effects of this exercise are strong, and they upload quickly to help you shift to a more desired mind-set. Eventually just hearing the sound will trigger the calm.

TOP-DOWN SOUND CUE

As we've discussed, reflection presets your awareness. So I recommend reflecting on how specific annoying sounds have affected your focus, organization, or disposition in the past. Ask: What can I learn from these past experiences? What should I do differently? Making yourself aware first will preset your mind's attentional process of inhibiting distracting sounds and activating those that may balance or energize. Consider using a top-down sound cue, like the sound of a deep breath, to keep you on task both when you visualize yourself in the situation you're trying to control and in real time. If you're in a private situation and it is appropriate to do so, sing a few bars of a song that sends the right message or play it for a moment on your phone or computer. Alternately, play it before and after the work circumstance you are attempting to condition.

TRY THIS!

You can use visualization to put preference on one environmental sound to help you inhibit or block another. Prior to an event you'd like to improve, such as taking a customer order, listening to directions, or discussing the vital details of a contract or business agreement, visualize any expected or predictable sound disturbances. Then imagine a pleasing sound that is actually part of that environment and that you think can override the disturbing sound. For example, you can choose white noise like the calming sound of a fan to deplete the noise of chatter, or light music to dissolve the sounds of a photocopier in a room next to yours. See yourself flowing and focused in the event as your pleasing sound washes out the predicted disturbing sound. Repeat the visualization a few times prior to the event. Your mind will follow course automatically in real time.

WHAT BEES CAN TEACH US ABOUT LEARNING AND MEMORY

In humans, what we learn affects our attention, as does motivation and memory. Insects demonstrate some similar functions. Bees, for example, also utilize memory, selectivity, learning, face recognition, and the ability to shift focus quickly from one learned target to another. In fact, bees can attend to some very complex things. They can learn to fly mazes, remember scents, and locate a faraway flower they are interested in. They can communicate to each other through what is known as a *waggle dance,* telling other bees where the most rewarding flowers might be. Honeybees can learn to recognize images of human faces.[12] Like human behaviors, bee behaviors are also affected by whether they are feeling optimistic or pessimistic. If, for instance, a bee has just been rewarded unexpectedly by a tasty, nutritious flower, it will slip into a dopamine-induced optimistic state and respond less aversively to a predator attack.

How does this translate to humans in the workplace? If you have work to do that requires careful judgment or analysis, then moments when you are on a dopamine high—a hormonal, emotional, and mental state triggered by receiving great news, for instance—are not the best time to pursue it. Same when your dopamine dipstick is low and you're feeling blah, depressed, or unrewarded. Again, you may want to hold off on important decision making in those moments. Remember, too, that you can practice any of your favorite mind-altering activities in this book to help you reset a dopamine imbalance.

Studies show bees can also learn from experience. For instance, they are able to modify their foraging behavior in response to experiences, suggesting the influence of both learning and memory in their selective discriminations. Bees can, for example, associate certain colors (as with flowers) with more favorable rewards or less favorable rewards. In fact, bees can do this faster than most animals. In a test to demonstrate this, bumblebees were able to avoid colors they had associated with an aversive quinine solution. Brains, even small ones, are wired to download rules from their environment for predicting the future, for memory storage, and for recall—effectively integrating a present situation with prior learning, memory, and actions for the best result.[13]

In humans, our increased cognitive muscle allows us finer, more complex forms of control and learning so we can create future scenarios that are consistent with our goals. For instance, we can manually spike up our alarm for existential details by using some of the wiring that makes us different from other animals. Looking back at Alex's story, we can see how he was able to control his urge to drop in on his boss by using reflection; connecting himself to a more vital, self-aware, goal-driven motivation; and self-generating a preset cue to support better actions. This is where human-level top-down control can count. If you place preset, goal-driven cues like "Stay with it or "Power through" in a time-related window (e.g., "as the meeting draws to an end" or "during the whole interview"), you can drive your attention to stay sharply on targets even when you're faced with distracters. I recommend starting today. I believe you'll enjoy the results.

WHAT WE CAN LEARN ABOUT REGRET FROM MICE

Behavioral neuroscientist Moriel Zelikowsky, PhD, studied the effects of social isolation in mice and discovered that they experience loneliness. What's more, she found that isolation generated a persistent fear in the mice, a fear that extended beyond that of the isolation itself. Loneliness also increased aggression.[14] According to Dr. Zelikowsky, humans don't need a ton of friends—just one will help lessen your loneliness.[15]

Mice can also have regret-like experiences, which they learn from. Importantly, such learning can result in long-term decision-making strategies toward future experiences.[16] Let's take a quick look at how this also applies to humans.

We have long known that humans attempt to avoid pain, regret, anxieties, and threats. But how can you turn regret into a positive action in the future? Let's say you waste your time arguing with a colleague over a trivial company policy during your lunch hour. Afterward you regret your argument. Upon reflection you learn how it contaminated the rest of your day and evening. Your regret and its lesson get stored in memory, which updates links to inform you next time you are in a similar situation and can guide you to reach for a more peaceful outcome. Reflection after each stage will update and ingrain the lesson further.

Here's another example of how you can use regret to your advantage. Let's say you are disappointed about failing to receive a promotion. Instead of drowning in your regret and settling into a self-defeating mind-set, you can visualize yourself getting the promotion next time and take positive steps to work toward that goal. When you take the time to reflect on how a situation may affect you, your goal, your career, and your personal satisfaction further down the line (e.g., in a month, in a year), you can transform your regret into a tool that ignites your motivation and inhibits potential negative aggressions, allowing you a chance to try to improve your skills. Sometimes associating what you initially view as an unrewarding situation with a personal, longer-range goal will allow you to transform regret into a more positive outlook.

Of course, there are also times where the avoidance of cause for regret is an appropriate strategy. For example, if you are a person who is prone to heartburn, a self-restricting word cue can help you avoid temptation: "If I eat one more of those donuts, I will get heartburn." This kind of avoidance can have good results if you need to be controlling your diet because of digestive or other health-related issues.

LIFELONG LEARNING AND
HOW WE CAN USE IT

Mice, like humans, show that they can transfer learning from one task to another. For example, Louis D. Matzel, PhD, found that mice that were trained in a working memory exercise improved their attention and learning abilities right away. Their performance also improved. What's more, improvements continued into older age in mice who had undergone lifelong working memory exercises. Experiments suggested that general impairments of learning, attention, and cognitive flexibility may be mitigated by a cognitive exercise regimen that requires chronic attentional engagement.[17]

In humans, this kind of learning transfer is important to all forms of self-improvement.

College students who regularly engage in vigorous exercise do better academically.[18] Additionally, martial arts and yoga are well-documented activities that improve attention.[19] Horseback riding, swimming and dance have also been found to improve attention.[20] Studies demonstrate that dance can cut back stress, increases levels of the feel-good hormone serotonin, and helps in the development new neural connections, especially in regions involved in executive function, long-term memory, and spatial recognition.[21] As a martial arts instructor for more than 20 years, I delightfully witnessed firsthand how students become more attentive and proficient in workplace, academic, and social activities in a parallel manner to their improvement in the dojo.

I want to emphasize that as learned behavioral algorithms (patterns) transfer from one task to another, a flowing, more rewarding mind-set results. You just have to learn how to hit your sweet spot in one situation and then you can transfer it to the next.

WHAT WE CAN LEARN ABOUT LEARNING FROM LARGE-BRAINED CREATURES

Dogs are a terrific example of what good can be achieved with goal-related learning. In one test to demonstrate how dogs pay attention, researchers found that compared to younger dogs, older dogs showed more calmness and were less affected by their environment as they tried to pay attention to details they were interested in. On the other hand, the younger dogs were able to pay attention longer. Both older and younger dogs effectively directed their attention when it involved something they wanted. The benefits of goal-related learning are not dismissed at any age.[22]

What else can we learn from dogs? Well, their propensity to be social gives them a learning advantage over some creatures. This is particularly observable in terms of learning what's safe. Dogs are amenable to learning from each other, and they learn from humans as well. Paying attention to others' reactions to and comfort levels with an object or place gives them a sense of its safety. When dogs sense a positive cue, then they approach.[23] This is called *social referencing*, and it is similar to our human experience.

Several years ago, I opened up a dialogue with colleagues on the idea of why intelligent people, at times, do unreasonable things. Sometimes these choices are harmful to the individuals and sometimes to others as well. We found that when others are doing the same thing, it's easy to give ourselves the green light. For example, if office supplies and equipment are allotted for office work only, yet everyone is taking all they want for personal home use, then individuals often interpret that behavior as okay. Let's up the ante: If enough of the organization's personnel are fudging travel requests to pay their fare for a holiday, then it's also easier for others to follow suit. Same with language biases as well as behavior that is discriminatory or inequitable. The list goes on and happens everywhere.

On the one hand, social referencing can advance learning. *What* we learn, however, can be another story. How we *apply* what we've learned can be yet another story. For instance, let's say you walk into a new job and you hear several employees commenting, trashing your supervisor. What lesson will you discover in the experience? Are you going to go for the surface easy "in" and play along with people you don't even know yet? Or are you going to sit back and figure out things for yourself?

Humans have the ability to preview and evaluate patterns that might shape our behavior. This type of visualization requires awareness and executive attention. In group situations, it is easy to follow suit. But this is where putting your attention on self-awareness, goal motivation, and next steps can help you create a better outcome.

TURNING ON THE PUPPY EYES—INTENTIONALLY?

If you love dogs, you've probably been swayed at one time or another by what is popularly referred to as *puppy eyes*. Do dogs intend to look at us so pleadingly? There is research suggesting yes. Perhaps they've evolved this skill from their drive to communicate with humans or from the reinforcement they get when we reward their appealing expression with whatever it is they want (e.g., food, drink, a walk outside on a warm day). Researchers have found that dogs display even more facial movement when we pay attention to them. This includes raising their eyebrows, making their eyes bigger, and showing their tongues.[24] All of these are forms of communication we have come to expect in our pets and enjoy. Does your dog actually know this about you? Very likely.

Dogs can recognize your facial expressions as well. Among other things, this tells them when you are paying attention to them, which of course they usually enjoy. In fact, research shows dogs prefer to take information from an attentive person.[25] This preference is an old and valuable tool exhibited in humans as well. In a way, it parallels our concept of the Golden Rule: Pay attention to others as you want them to pay attention to you.

Paying attention to colleagues, customers, and clients builds trust and other positive emotions. Add this pleasant skill to your tool kit. It feeds other people's natural way of learning in order to better know how to proceed with other individuals and with tasks. Makes good sense.

TRY THIS!

Sync an appropriate facial message with what you are saying to and hearing from another person. It makes a difference, and your communication and rapport will both improve. Try practicing this skill with a mirror. Imagine you are in the middle of an important scene. Ask yourself, "What message should my expression convey? Given the situation and our mutual goals, how will the other person perceive my expression?" This exercise will help you sharpen your delivery because it will allow you to explore your options and choose the best approach for the way you wish to portray yourself.

Sometimes a little inspiration is needed to start things off. I recommend visualizing people you know who are really good at this skill. Ask yourself, "What facial expressions can I adapt from their repertoire? Consider several. Think: eyes, posture, smile, hand gestures, and the like. How would they present themselves to someone we were about to meet with face to face?" Start with adjusting your body language just a tiny bit before exploring more expressive communication. Consider how you want to be perceived—attentive, personable, interested. You can make up your own list. Try your new skill out on someone outside of your workplace experience and then take it on the road.

SOUND: THE STRONGEST MIND-ALTERING INFLUENCERS OF MENTAL STATES

Elephants, like humans and many other animals, frequently rely on sound. Put to the test, elephants can distinguish age, gender, and even ethnicity by hearing the sound of someone's voice. Their close sensitivity to sound helps them identify existential threats, [26] and they even use sound to comfort one another when they are distressed. In fact, sound is one of the most powerful mind-altering influencers of mental states. Have you ever gone straight to your car after a rough day and immediately tuned in to Adele, David Matthews, or the Stones to sponge away the bummer? You may have other favorite musicians, but you get the point. The comforting powers of sound and music are loved by humans and are perhaps nothing short of a gift from the gods.

Historically, sound was perceived as the first medicine, and that still holds clout today. The Greek deity Apollo, the god of music and medicine, is recognized as the original resource for health and healing and is listed first in the *Hippocratic Oath*, which is recited by graduating medical students across the land even today.[27] The Greek philosopher and mathematician Pythagoras, who lived from 570 through 490 BC, was fascinated with the power of sound, maintaining that sound was subject to mathematical calculation throughout the universe. A stunning example of his calculations is his measurement of notes on a one-stringed instrument called a *monochord*. Although he lacked modern technology, his measurements of musical intervals were perfect and hold unto this day. But he didn't stop there. He hypothesized that sound vibrations can have an effect on all things in the universe, including the organs within the body.

Sound is very important to attention training. As a developing embryo, you were surrounded by the sounds of your mother's heartbeat, placenta, and umbilical cord. You understood these sounds internally, organically. Your mind and body responded to it. This is because the core features of sound and music are the same as those of the brain: *rhythm, amplitude, resonance, dissonance,* and *synchrony.* As such, this magic elixir can make changes in your physical and mental states—and fast. Consequently, it is one of the favorite "medicines" of human beings.

Using sound for comfort is universal. *Motherese,* which can be defined as the cooing sounds that parents make for infants to comfort them, ease their distress, or make them happier is one example. Universally, no matter what the parents' native language, this often involves vowel sounds: o-o-o-hs and a-h-hs, and w-e-e-es.

One of your strongest assets for self-transformation is your ability to consciously combine the tools of sound, preawareness, and attention to other sensory details and intentionally preset and strengthen them in your behavior through self-awareness, visualization, and reflection. At this point, such a conscious regimen appears to be uniquely yours. Trust it. Use it often.

CHAPTER EXERCISES

Learning from Important Experiences

This exercise allows you to take advantage of the way your mind automatically updates how to think, feel, and act in key experiences and how it saves the updated links to guide your behaviors in the future whenever you find yourself in similar experiences. All you have to do is find a quiet and appropriate time to reflect on your experience afterward. You can do this later in the day or even the next day. Here are the steps.

1. Envision the entire environment and scene in which the experience occurred.
2. Ask what you initially wanted from the situation. Boost your mindfulness so that you can see clearly into your original intentions.
3. Next, ask, "Did I achieve my intention? What helped? Is there anything others would want me to do differently? Is there anything I'd do differently in the future?"
4. If you would do something differently, visualize yourself in the same environment and scenario engaging these new behaviors. Take your time seeing how they would work out. Edit the behaviors where necessary and remember to make flexibility part of your strategy toward similar future situations.
5. Revisit this imagined scenario prior to a comparable upcoming experience.

Associating Sound with a Specifically Desired Mind-State

This exercise utilizes the components of self, movement, environment, sound, and memory.

1. Pick one upcoming situation you'd like to have better control over.
2. Remind yourself what your overall goal is. Ask yourself, "Why is this goal important?"
3. Pick the most important behavior you need to ensure you perform well. Ask yourself, "Why is this specific behavior so important?"
4. Identify a song you love (lyrical or instrumental) that emphasizes the specific behavior you've identified.
5. Place the song on your cell phone or other electronic device and use it as a soundtrack as you visualize yourself in the situation. Hear the message your song is delivering. See it shaping your actions in the expected environment. See yourself from all angles, especially from the perspective of others. Edit your behaviors if necessary. As you make edits, you may wish to change the sound message you are sending yourself and to choose a more situationally appropriate song.
6. When the visualization and soundtrack successfully sync with and guide your best behaviors, use them randomly and often in the days before the event and then again immediately before and after the event. Tweak after if needed.

Training Your Desired Mind-Set with Imagery

Like the previous exercise, this also utilizes the components of self, movement, environment, imagery, and memory.

1. Imitating Ali's *"Float like a butterfly, sting like a bee"* mantra, create a similar one-line power phrase to guide your actions, thoughts, and feelings in a specific upcoming event.
2. Prior to the actual event, visualize yourself in it as if in a mind-movie. Intersperse your mantra/power phrase throughout the scene. See yourself from all angles, especially from the perspective of others as your mantra sharpens your performance.
3. Edit both your mantra and behaviors if necessary.
4. When the image successfully syncs with and guides your behaviors, repeat the visualization.
5. Repeat randomly and often in the days before the event and then again immediately before and after the event. Tweak after if needed.

6

A Glance Is All You Need...Sometimes

Rule #6

Widen your attentional spotlight regularly to help catch important peripheral data.

Remember when your teachers used to tell you they could keep tabs on you because they had eyes in the back of their head? In a funny way, they were right. You have probably experienced being at a work-related seminar or something of the kind and directing your attention to the front of the room. Suddenly there is a loud noise from an adjacent room. You instantly abandon your focus and turn your attention toward the intruding, *peripheral* sound. Can the automatic brain function that so quickly derailed you in one circumstance be a great tool in another?

Also called *glance information* or *gist*, this information-gathering mechanism is wired into your attention network and you can take advantage of its capabilities. You can, in fact, take in a lot of information in just a simple glance and at very high speed. And you can do more with it than you may think. All it takes is one eye movement, one sound bite or one hint of other sensory data. This allows you quick access to external images and sounds and other sensual information or to—in a glance—shift your attention internally to recognize what's going on inside you that may be influencing your momentary performance. That can include memories of similar experiences as well as any physical or emotional feelings (e.g., you may feel hungry or frustrated or overconfident). Knowing how and when to open your focus to fringe details helps you get the most from this intriguing faculty. Like so much of what we know about focus, however, understanding how to use gist includes seeing its two sides—that is, determining when it is advantageous and when it is not.

We live in a society where so much seems to happen in a glance—from tweets to texts to checking the stock market on your cell phone's home screen. It's as if technology is helping us train this function. It only takes milliseconds, in fact, for you to take a glance and process new information. Filmmakers have entertained us by appealing to this ability for years with techniques like montage, which uses slices of scenes to create a mosaic of images that can tell the story of years in seconds. For instance, the artistically acclaimed film *Run Lola Run*[1] exploited this technique with lightning-fast cuts delivered in milliseconds that were able to generate high drama.

You can usually capture visual gist during first eye contact. For example, during a Kansas State University experiment to test imagery, researchers flashed pictures at individuals at very high speeds. The researchers determined that in just milliseconds, people could recognize whether the images showed a beach scene, dining room, or a street scene.[2]

Furthermore, sound and other sensory information can also be recognized and have their effects on you in milliseconds.

Consider this scenario. A waiter walks across a restaurant carrying a tray of entrées. You glance at him and turn your attention back to the conversation at your table. You then hear the sound of wood and metal banging together. Without even looking, you have the sense of knowing pretty instantly what just happened: the waiter bumped into a chair. All it took was one earlier glance to know that a table in his path was empty, as were the chairs.

Research continues to determine with more specificity what we visually pay attention to on the fringe. The three basic elements we tend to mentally scan for are objects, descriptive detail, and spatial relations. An example is clouds over a beach with a horizon in the distance.[3] Your scanning ability relies upon other capacities, like your previous learning and memory, including emotional memories. These elements work together and allow you to establish predictions and expectations.

Let's say you glance at an unfamiliar photo and see a dark spot in the center of a beach image. Other information you have downloaded converges, creating a context that may or may not be unique to you. In this case, past information and experiences allow you to identify the dark spot as a boat. A series of dark images in the center of the street scene, however, might prompt you to identify them as motor vehicles. Another person with different learning, feelings, and experiences could perceive a different context. Also, not all of our quick glances are correct. For example, a glanced image of a plastic grocery bag that fell off the counter onto your kitchen floor may lead you to make the false conclusion that it's your cat if the bag appears in the very spot where your cat usually lounges on the floor in the sun.

Sound works similarly. For example, many of us know all too well the unfortunate sound of a fender bender. Once you've heard it, you tend to connect the sound to the accident instantly.

Although your ability to discern information from a glance may go awry (as in the cat example), it can also help you sidestep a potentially big problem. For instance, let's say you are driving through an intersection with a green light. Out of the corner of your eye, you suddenly see that a pedestrian is about to step off the sidewalk to cross in front of you. You screech to a stop, no doubt avoiding an accident. An amazing aspect of gist is that it seems to be able to prioritize fringe information in your mind. This allows you to cut through distracters to sustain or reset your focus, as when you screech to a halt instead of proceeding through the intersection with the green light.

Consider the following story of Roslyn, an acquaintance of mine who worked at an all-night minimarket. One evening, when she was the only employee in the store, a customer entered. She didn't spot anything particularly noticeable about him until he approached her at the counter. Then she saw that he had a handgun, which he aimed directly at her. He demanded whatever cash was on hand. She, of course, cooperated. Even so, the gunman took a shot at her, at point-blank range. Fortunately, he missed, and then he fled. Later, I asked her how it was that he had missed. She said she didn't really know for sure, but that she had dropped to the floor in a split second, at "apparently just the right time." She concluded that it must have been just as he shot.

"I saw something out of the corner of my eye," she told me. "Some movement in his hand or arm—something—and I automatically hit the ground."

She added, with humble amazement, that only later did she realize that the bullet had hit the wall right behind where she was standing. Maybe he intentionally missed; maybe not. Either way, her reaction was spot on.

The baseball world is filled with examples of catchers using no more than a glance to pick off players jetting off first base to steal second. Similarly, runners and swimmers often know in a glance exactly when to really pour it on during a competition. Take, for instance, the Omaha 2016 Olympic Trials, in which Michael Phelps faced his strongest competition from his long-time friend Ryan Lochte. Having challenged each other three times already in the trials, Lochte and Phelps were down to the last race. On the final turn of the race, Phelps had a slight lead. ESPN reported it this way: "Phelps looked out of the corner of his eye. He saw Lochte. He knew he held a slim advantage."[4] Kicking with all he had, Phelps touched the wall first, winning by one-third of a second. It was the last time the two would compete against one another in the US with the 2016 Olympics fast in sight.[5]

Gist also applies to feelings. In the workplace, this capability can manifest itself as a fringe feeling—like the subtle feeling that you need to give yourself more time to finish a project that is taking longer than you thought. Though such a feeling may only last seconds, it may be sending you an important message.

Consider the following example: Tucker is a communication services specialist. It was a Saturday afternoon and he was writing an article for his organization's upcoming Employee Development Day workshops. He was determined to get the blurb to his assistant to batch email by 3:00 p.m., even though it didn't have to go out until Monday morning. Tucker could feel his attention to the piece waning. He initially thought he could just sail through writing it and finish early, but that wasn't happening. In the back of his mind was an academic paper he needed to complete for an after-work class he was taking to complete his MBA. He knew the paper would require longer time and would be the culmination of years of work. Every few minutes he'd get a flash feeling, the gist of which was that he needed to shift from the Development Day announcement and put his energies on his college paper—for the benefit of both projects. Ignoring the gist of his feelings and resolved to send the itinerary on to his assistant, he emailed a rough draft of the article. In his rush he forgot to say that it was a rough draft, and his assistant batch mailed it for all to see the name of the previous year's keynote speaker, who was now unfortunately deceased. He had not removed the name when he copy-pasted formats from the previous year's workshops in order to speed things up. In such situations gist feelings may be spot on or possibly not. Still, I recommend using them to your advantage by hitting the pause button. Move them into your main focus, even if only momentarily. Ask yourself what is the measure of risk in making a decision without more thought? Is there benefit? Is there liability? These are legitimate concerns.

Sometimes an introspective glance (millisecond) can be all you need to guide you back on the track that is best for you. Here's how.

TRY THIS!

Next time you are involved in a task, take a quick internal glance to determine whether you are feeling comfortable, confident, and correct in your approach or whether you are experiencing a flash feeling that your actions are off base. If the latter feeling exists, take a moment's pause. Ask yourself, "What is my specific goal here? Do I want to change anything in my immediate strategy?" If so, rethink the issue and then return to the project when your concern has been cleared. If there is nothing that needs changing, then take a moment to absorb your confidence and the burst of positive energy it issues. Amplify this feeling with any of the mindfulness-boosting exercises from this book, then head back into your project with invigorated buoyancy.

WHERE MEANING COMES FROM

We conclude meaning from situations so quickly, we usually aren't aware of how we are getting to that meaning. However, our rapid-fire conclusions can influence the way an entire experience turns out. In a glance, you can catch an entire scene: objects, sounds, feelings, and even your thoughts about it. From this combination of "scene" and previous experience, you conclude meaning. Your mind is linking your past memory with learning that you have gleaned from previous actions in similar scenarios or tasks. You weigh stored details against your current goal and environment. You narrow the spotlight of your focus until it reaches a specific context. The process is dynamic: you scan detail, weigh in previous information, come to conclusions, and repeat.

For example, let's say you are in your living room when peripherally you hear the closing of the dishwasher door in your kitchen, followed by a clanging metal sound. Although you can't see what's actually happening, you remember that you made cookies that morning, and you conclude that the sound is the result of a couple of baking sheets banging into each other in the dishwasher. A similar sound coming from underneath your car, however, could indicate a loose shield or other metallic part. In that case, you may conclude that the vehicle requires a visit to your mechanic.

Because much of my time is spent in the Berkshires, I am quite familiar with the sounds of that rural environment. So, for example, it is common to hear the crackling sound of fireworks, especially during the summer. Yet I've also learned that they generally disappear during other seasons—especially spring. During that season, when I hear similar sounds, I realize that they are gunshots from a rifle sporting range across the mountaintop. The context that generates this conclusion is primarily spatial as well as chronological. I know where the range is and the time of day the range operates.

A few summers ago, a friend of mine from New York City visited me in the Berkshires for the first time. He became quite concerned about potential gunfire one evening because he wasn't able to put a rural context to the sounds he was hearing (they were actually fireworks). In this way, associations, expectations, predictions, and conclusions rely highly on personal memory and context. However, as with most automatic functions, there is no guarantee of accuracy or of what's best in a certain situation. If you fail to get clear about how one situation's context may differ from another, you can develop or ignore serious problems in any goal pursuit. Making assumptions without pausing for clarification is one possible reason for stress and compulsive behaviors.

You can use mindfulness and self-awareness to intervene against stress and compulsivity. These tools will help you self-regulate, and they can enhance your process at all levels. It makes sense to tap this regimen as soon as you begin feeling signs of discomfort, misdirection, or conflict. Pause and ask yourself questions such as these: "Do my previous conclusions about this circumstance currently apply? Is there anything different in context now? How does that change my conclusions?" Answers to these questions can help you put your focus where it will do the most good.

TRY THIS!

Next time you are in a one-on-one discussion with a fellow professional or are making a presentation at a larger gathering, consider using literal imagery that the audience will relate to. To help you choose images that will make your point most effectively, ask yourself, "Who are the people in my audience? Gender? Age? Background? Lifestyle?" Select imagery that can resonate with them via their experiences but that is also authentically shared by you. Consider this technique to enhance your PowerPoints.

WORDS

The convergence of contextual details, which also come together in a flash, is also important to language. For instance, when you hear a homonym like *prey* (versus *pray*) or *hi* (versus *high*), you can figure out in milliseconds which meaning is intended from the context of the conversation, even though you can't see the actual spelling. For example, if you hear me say that "people like to pray at church," you can tell the meaning of *pray* by its reference to the rest of the sentence.

A friend was recently discussing demographics with a coworker, and she used the term *sects*. As part of the conversation, her coworker responded, "What sects are you relying on most?" Another colleague, who overheard them, said, "What are you two talking about over there?" This serves as a humorous lesson that sometimes we need more context to accurately conclude anything.

As far as language is concerned, tone is another factor that ultimately gives your words meaning. For example, if you text me asking how my weekend went and I simply write down "great," you don't really know how it went. Without hearing my tone, you can't be sure if I'm being sarcastic or not. In fact, it could be just the opposite of what "great" usually implies.

Sometimes in writing, typography can effectively substitute for tone. For instance, if I write *"GREAT!"* you get a better handle on how I mean it. Consider the difference between the following lines: *I can't eat there* and *I can't eat **there***. The latter hints that there may be something wrong with the establishment. Usually, it is easiest to pick up these types of distinctions when we hear words said aloud.

A few years ago I conducted a survey among 20-somethings to identify the most annoying commercial that was being aired throughout a specific metropolitan area. As it turned out, they chose the most unpopular one not because of the content but because of the narrator's tone, which they described as insincere and not to be trusted. In fact, one survey respondent indicated that just a split second of the narrator's voice was enough to make him reach out to turn off the radio. As we've discussed throughout the book, those kinds of experiences provide our mind with guidance links to future similar experiences.

As indicated in the last chapter, tones can also be used to comfort as well as to alert others. Be sure to adjust your tone as needed for specific situations. Use tone to your advantage to better deliver your gist so that your coworkers and other professionals don't arrive at conflicting and inaccurate conclusions that could stand in the way of your hitting your goals.

BODY LANGUAGE

As we discussed earlier, you will also want to take care to choose appropriate body language and facial expressions. With just a quick glance, people rapidly conclude whether or not a face in a crowd is untrustworthy.[6] Hauntingly, we tend to remember those faces that are incongruent with our expectations in a moment or event (e.g., the face of someone who surprised us by turning out to be untrustworthy).[7] Actors in commercials, individuals in sales, and people in all customer-related activities need to put attention on this element. Remember that people are reading our facial and body language at the same time we are trying to read theirs. This will bear influence on how we behave toward and trust each other in the future.

In chapter 3, we looked at how Frank's negative associations of his father's body language lived unconsciously in his head and impacted his present-day decisions. All it took now was a glance at similar body movements and Frank was ready to give up on a work goal he really wanted. Luckily for Frank, he saw the trigger for the ball-and-chain hindrance it was. He caught it by effectively practicing self-awareness and mindful reflecting. That regiment can also help you to inhibit—and eventually do away with—the influence of specific, harmful fringe information. Reflection, self-awareness, and mindfulness will help you dig out negative triggers even if they have become unconscious to you. To ensure that they don't keep sweeping you further and further from your goals, I recommend starting today.

SCAN THE GIST OF YOUR COMFORT ZONES

Today, science accepts the fact that the mind can have significant influence over the way our body is operating and vice versa. This idea has been prominent in my own personal development and work as a researcher. The mind-body connection is, however, a two-way street: the body can bear its influence over an otherwise fatigued, depressed, or dysfunctioning mind (e.g., an improvement of mood after exercise) just as a lethargic, stressed, or negative mind-state can bear its influence adversely on an otherwise healthy body (e.g., with tension headaches or other aches and pains). Optimally, you can recognize these moments before they fully set in—when you are *almost* in their throes—and you can shift before they get to you, using your body to balance your mind and vice versa. If either is out of balance, then reaching a state of flow is impossible.

You can use your attention machinery to increase your body intelligence and its balancing capabilities. Your success will depend on your ability to scan the gist of your comfort zones, because you can't constantly be concentrating on them. Let's discuss a few more examples.

Externally, your comfort zones are affected by your senses. For example, perhaps seeing or wearing earth tones calms you down or reds lift your energy. Take a moment and consider what colors are your favorite calmers and energizers. Pick an outfit for tomorrow by matching colors with the mental energy you think you will need to help keep your mind more attentive and flowing.

Internally, your comfort zones are associated with feelings or emotions. Become more sensitive to these interior zones by asking yourself questions like these: "What feelings are getting in the way of a task or of a communication with a certain client? What emotions are blocking me from tackling the mound of paperwork I need to finish by the end of the day?"

One way to achieve this kind of sensitivity and balance is to scan your internal affective zones and consider if they facilitate where you are at the moment. You can expand your scan to include physical feelings. Ask yourself, "Am I running on low energy? Am I tense? Am I feeling butterflies in my stomach? Is there pain anywhere in my body?" These steps give you a window of opportunity to recharge, rebalance, and regain control.

Externally, you can ask yourself questions like these: "Am I warm? Cold? Do I have enough light? Do I need more quiet? Do I need a neater workspace?" When your comfort zones are running on empty, it is difficult to maintain good attention and focus. With a little practice, a simple glance will give you the calculations you need to self-regulate.

Your executive attention machinery allows you to overrule immediate irrelevant urges and to give more attention to identifiable needs, like upping your mental and/or physical energy or balancing off an interfering emotional interference. As we've noted, it is best if you can catch such conflicts prior to when they become chronic. The key is to learn to be familiar with your own warning signs and to keep tabs on them in a glance.

When you are considering how you feel in a given moment, consider your anxiety level. It's well known that we need a certain amount of anxiety to perform our best, yet it's a delicate balance. Just a bit more anxiety can have a strong enough negative effect to veer you off of task-required details. Here, too, the good news is that you can do something about it. In a glance, you can also capture the details signaling your anxiety. Being aware of and sensitive to your affective zone's early signals allows you to control them.

Remember that humans have the unique ability to visualize and choose, using information from multiple areas affecting our mind. You can additionally generate top-down cues to bias the way your mind is functioning by scanning your emotions, memory, external details, and current task; determining how you are feeling generally and specifically; and identifying whether you should be first addressing any of these subsystems affecting your performance before going forward any further. Then proceed with what is most advantageous in your scenario.

 You brain's gisting capability allows you to take in a lot of sensory information in just fractions of a second. Use this information to scan your internal and external zones regularly and to keep them in balance with your goals.

CHAPTER EXERCISES

Scanning for Imbalance

Sometimes a glance may be all you need to get back into a flowing mind. If you are having difficulty staying in the flow of a task, take a fast glimpse at what is affecting you externally and internally.

1. Ask yourself, "What appears relevant and should be addressed? What is irrelevant?
2. Has your assessment of relevancy or irrelevancy suddenly come about? Why?
3. Do you want to change anything in how you are approaching your task?" Give it all a second look and focus on identifying any distracters interrupting your flowing mind-set. Consider when these should be addressed and then how you will do so.

Later, use reflection to adjust and learn how you might do things differently next time to avoid these distracters. This will imbed techniques and actions and link them to future endeavors so that you will automatically avoid similar problems.

Speaking in Public and Using PowerPoints

Musicians, actors, and professional public speakers rely on being able to determine how engaged their audience is, whether the audience is grasping the important parts of the presentation, and what the audience is most responding to. With some practice, you can make these determinations too. When giving your next talk, try to notice in a glance if individuals are engaged. You can also see what details they engage with most.

If you are in a larger room that requires a podium, try moving about the room, at least up to the first row of seating. You might even feel comfortable walking to the back or side of the room for a short moment. Try to make eye contact with sections of audience. It only takes a glance. If you notice someone positively connecting, you can even talk directly to that person when a detail applies directly to him or her.

You can also be more conversational if you utilize imagery in your PowerPoint and lessen text. This way, a quick glance at the imagery on screen is all you'll need to compose your narrative. As we've discussed, the best images are those that are within your audience's experiences as well as within yours. The best eye contact is the kind you make when you're having a meal with a close friend and talking about a mutually meaningful idea.[8]

I always recommend using reflection after a presentation. This helps you see where things worked and where they didn't so you can adjust for next time.

7

How Did I Miss That? It Was Right in Front of My Nose

Rule #7

Strengthen your attention span.

Bill is an administrator for a city arts center. Late one Sunday night, he was finalizing edits on a grant application that was due by the end of the next day. Too tired to think clearly any longer, and having just a few changes left to make on the application, he called it quits and hit the proverbial sack. The next morning, he pushed the snooze button on his cell phone several times before getting out of bed. He would have loved another hour of sleep, but that wasn't going to happen. As the morning progressed, one thing led to another. Life became hectic. The grant slipped further down Bill's to-do list. And that afternoon, when he finally had a moment to think more freely again, he remembered that part of it still needed editing—but he couldn't remember which parts needed more work. Fatigue from the late night before and his busy day had left him feeling mentally and energetically glitched. He scrolled the application a few times but still couldn't locate anything to jog his memory about the edits. To make things worse, his stress over finishing the application on time was increasing. With time slipping away, he made an executive decision, pushed the send key, and sped the application on its way without the edits, hoping for the best.

Many of us, under similar pressures, have experienced scenarios like Bill's. We justify our predicaments with slogans like, "You do what you have to do." Then we muscle through, hoping for the best.

Like Bill, you may often find that your attention fluctuates like a radio signal from strong to good or fair and sometimes weak. It's easy for your attention to unexpectedly conk out and your memory to freeze. Sometimes you just feel cloudy upstairs, like you are trying to find your way through a fog.

As humans, we are pretty adaptive, but sometimes this capacity hurts more than helps. As our energy runs down, we may adapt by cutting corners, hurrying tasks, and making choices that are not really in our best interest. Sometimes we fail to notice certain task-related details, facts, objects, concepts, communications, and interpersonal choices—even when they are right in front of our nose. Even as we are unable to see important details, we may emphatically be attracted to irrelevant details—derailing ourselves twice as we work toward the goal.

Fatigue makes it easy for mistakes to occur because memory circuits shut down. As such, so do links in our memory to the way we may have handled things formerly in a successful manner. Our ability to organize also takes a hit. We tend to choose inadequate or sometimes incorrect actions. As these elements interact with each other, it's easy for the cycle to start feeding itself into a downward spin.

Ever place a cup of coffee on your desk, forget you did so,

and then knock it all over important paperwork? Or discover some unintended word rolling out of your mouth, unable to put the brakes on it? The worlds of public speaking and broadcast media offer many humorous examples of gaffs—as well as some not-so-funny ones. In fact, gaffs in live media are so common that you can find (and even subscribe to) a plethora of comical bloopers online. One of my favorite is from a weather announcer who attempts to segue from the news to her segment. During the broadcast, which is live, she starts out by saying on camera, "Details looking at your next shhhit—" then pauses as she catches the gaff, corrects herself, and continues.

"CHANCE," she says, emphasizing the right word. "CHANCE of some rain." She laughs heartily and adds, "Ooh, that was close!"[1]

In the same compilation of bloopers, an anchor on another show spills his coffee over his desk and over his cohost, too. And yet another anchor trips over a box while walking across the studio live, on air. The pitch of her voice rises as she exclaims, "Who-o-o-p, did you guys see that? That was on TV, right?" Then she laughs as she continues on her way.[2]

All institutions suffer from gaffs. When I talk about these flub-ups at presentations, people love to tell of their own mistakes with a touch of humor and humility. Of course, although many of our examples are light, this isn't to say such blips always are humorous; at times, they can be out-and-out painful. Ask any politician, educator, or businessperson.

So, what can steal your attention so fast you make a big blunder? Automatizations, as we have been discussing, are at the top of the list. But remember that when these circuits are working to your advantage, they are also pretty useful. However, before we explore how they specifically deplete or strengthen your attention, I want to discuss how a few other factors steal your attention span. These include stress, emotional factors, your body's hormonal activity, and something that may seem fairly harmless—individual beliefs—which nonetheless steal your attention in a split second. You will notice by this chapter's end that all four affect your memory and that each of these elements interacts with the others. When they do, the strength of their ability to influence you increases even further. As a result, your job in Rule 7 is to eliminate their negative influence and use their positive effects to sustain a mind-set that is advantageous to your goals.

ENERGY VAMPIRES

You can't pay attention to much when you lack energy, and you can't do anything well when you lack the right energy. A certain amount of energy is necessary, for instance, to maintain good working memory, to process information, and to concentrate. You need energy to simply feel good. But your body's energy resources are not unlimited. No one can, as such, operate in any one mind-set—say, analytical—endlessly. The pipeline will run out and your risks of making errors will multiply. To prevent this, you need to keep your energy consumption in check to ensure that your mental and physical energy reserves have enough quality energy for the tasks you undertake. How much? In part, this will depend on the task and on you. For instance, it takes a different type and amount of energy to bench press 350 pounds as compared to solving a difficult math problem or playing the piano.

As a gauge, I offer you this: As you feel your energy reserves dip below about 80 percent, consider it time to shift from your energy consumption mode to your energy cultivation mode. At 80 percent, dissatisfaction and irritation start coming on, and you're better off pausing to restore your balance. Part of our job in attention training is expanding our energy cultivating tool-box. This shift offers immediate relief, giving your reserve tank a fill and keeping you motivated, on course, and in the flow. You can do this with any of the techniques mentioned in this book. They will fit a wide variety of situations and will keep your good energy flowing all day.

WHEN STRESSORS DRAIN YOU LIKE THERE'S NO END IN SIGHT

Stress is one of the largest consumers of your overall energy. It messes with your attention span and with your ability to focus on what's important in the moment, resulting in blunders and more stress.

As indicated in the introduction of this book, Gallup reported that people in the United States are among the most stressed individuals worldwide. According to their research, "55% were said to feel stressed during the day, 45% felt worried a lot, and more than one in five (22%) said they felt anger a lot."[3] Stress is the result of prolonged tension, and sometimes it feels like there's no end in sight. However, I'm here to tell you it can be cleared out of your attentional beam.

First, a little background. Stress is a two-way street. It alters your body's electrochemical, biological, and psychological activity. Then each of these circles back and affects the intensity of the stress you feel, which means that unchecked stress becomes a vicious circle.

Let's consider your body's electrical activity. Stress both affects and is affected by your brain waves, which are electrical currents in your brain. One way your brain organizes itself into calm or aroused states is by changing the velocity of your brain waves, making them run quicker or slower. Higher velocities are associated with awake, excited, and stress states; lower velocities are associated with calm, sleep, and dream states. By increasing or decreasing brain wave frequencies, your brain can reach various levels of calmness or alertness. Self-regulating this activity can play a significant role in sustaining a strong attention span. The good news is that you can self-regulate this process.

From highest to lowest frequency, your brain waves are called *beta, alpha, theta,* and *delta.* The high beta range is associated with high mental arousal, which you might experience in a moment of intense concentration. Unfortunately, because beta waves are also associated with feelings of stress, anxiety, and fight-or-flight responses, they can send you into your nervous zones as well. In contrast, alpha waves are slower. These are associated with a relaxed, attentive, and alert mind-state. Linked to states of mindfulness, alpha waves can stimulate faster, more confident decision making as well as put your mind in a good place for creative thinking. Theta waves are slower still. These are associated with a mind-state between sleep and wakefulness. Delta waves are your slowest waves. They are associated with deep, dreamless sleep.

Which mind-state is best? When you are working on an intense mathematical calculation, your alpha and theta waves naturally go down and your beta waves go up to give you sharper concentration. So it depends on what you need in a certain moment. But sometimes—due to low energy, stress, and other factors—you need to self-regulate this process. Left unattended, it is easy to get caught in a loop of lower energy, more stress, blunders, emotional fatigue, and so on. Attention training is about turning this negative energy loop off and then willfully sending your brain waves up or down to meet your goals with the best mind-state.

Let's look at how stress affects this physio-psychological activity. Stress can be understood as a type of psychological and physical pain, experienced when we feel threatened or too inadequate to deal with people and situations. It's a common experience, like when you worry that a mole that suddenly appeared on your chest is cancer, or that the headaches you've suffered through mean a brain tumor. No one sets out to get stressed; it just happens.

As such, stress is also guided by your *perception* of pressure. For example, when you are facing a deadline you might feel overwhelmed, whereas your colleague, under similar pressure, might enjoy racing against the clock. The work and the deadline are the same, but your perceptions differ. When you are stressed, you are draining energy and depleting your attention span.

It's a bit of a balancing act. For example, some levels of stress actually help us deal with uncertainties and challenges in life. Consider a baseball player on first base who is thinking about stealing second base. He catches a glimpse of an unexpected throw to the first baseman in an attempt to pick him off. In an instant, his brain issues a stream of adrenaline, the fight-or-fight hormone, through his bloodstream. His pulse, blood pressure, and breathing increase. These send more oxygen into his brain and muscles, which helps him make the steal.

In fact, adrenaline's everyday effects can go even further. They heighten your focus and memory, linking them together to better enhance performance. Adrenaline also reduces pain. It makes actions, whether physical or mental, feel more effortless. Sport competitions are full of examples of athletes who performed amazingly on an adrenaline rush despite injuries such as broken bones or muscle damage.

On the other hand, too much of this hormone will cripple performance. Stress left uncontrolled will consume the physical and mental energy you need to manage your day in a flowing state. It will leave you fatigued and vulnerable to weakened thinking, feelings, and decision making. Anyone who has ever taken a test has experienced moments when the mind just freezes. One reason is that when adrenaline is not enough, another of your body's hormones, cortisol, kicks in. Involved in your body's healthy response to stress, a certain amount of cortisol, like adrenaline, is necessary for peak performance and for maintaining good focus. However, if the valve stays open too long, cortisol turns on you, so to speak, interfering with your ability to process, organize, and recall information. Too much cortisol can lower your self-esteem and cause you to lose confidence. Like a deer caught in headlights, you may find that cortisol in excess can cause you to freeze or choke at a crucial moment. Again, balance is key.

When you're stressed, you don't often—if ever—stop to smell the proverbial roses. This is because as a side effect, stress sweeps your attention away from the positive energy influencers all around you. Cutting off the simple positive energies in your world makes it more difficult to navigate it. You wind up meeting grind with more grind, and it's difficult to keep this pattern up without burning out. You walk away more fatigued, with less energy in your reserves. This becomes a formula for further workplace, academic, social, or familial problems.

One thing you can do to rebalance your energy is widen your focus. Reopen it to include positive environmental influencers. You need to see positivity in your world. You need to know it is within your reach. From the perspective of positive psychology, sometimes all you have to do is look out the window.

Another possible way to achieve some relief is to change your modus operandi from an energy consumption mind-state that leaves you stressed to one that promotes energy cultivation. Music and natural sounds are my favorite methods.

TRY THIS!

Listening to music or recorded natural sounds like a powerful waterfall or a gentle breeze are great tools to help you reverse stress and fill up your energy reserves with more balanced energy. To begin, focus your attention internally to help you identify whether your stress is coming from a feeling of too low energy—e.g., you feel you don't have adequate energy to successfully complete your task—or if your stress is coming from having too much. Then depending on the type of energy you need to balance, locate a tune or a natural sound that you feel will have the arousing or calming effect. To make this work, you need to choose something you truly like that fits your goal. For example, a thunderous waterfall or loud, bawdy, quick-paced metal tune, if it's your thing, can spike your energy for a bench press, while a gentle breeze or Mozart sonata might steady your nerves as you prepare to tackle a mathematical equation. Along the same lines, a tune by Enya might calm you as you prepare for bed. Place your chosen tune on your cell phone so that you have it whenever you need to feel more relaxed. Then push play whenever you need its healthy beats.

REDUCE HEAD CLUTTER AND STRENGTHEN ATTENTION SPAN

How many times a day do you feel like you have too much on your mind? Something inside us organically knows this state weakens our attentional signal.

Relaxation can offer some immediate relief. It doesn't take much. Talking a brief walk, looking out the window, or doing some light meditation might be all you need to revitalize.

Getting more organized can also help you deal with the clutter in your mind. For instance, you can strategize one or more possible ways to navigate an upcoming experience; this approach will help you cut out distracting details as the event approaches. Consider incorporating this skill daily, but don't make your plan so airtight that it turns into a leash around your neck. Feeling you have some flexibility in strategy is important toward reducing stress.

Consider having a most important daily goal when you enter your workspace—just for the purpose of cutting down head clutter. You can remind yourself of your goal randomly throughout the day to help you focus on what matters. I'm a big fan of using the cell phone in a variety of ways to generate all kinds of positive mind-sets. One easy way to do this is to make yourself a Post-it reminder and save it to your cell phone; you can also send yourself a text or an email that states the goal. There are several terrific apps you might like to check out, such as Microsoft's Sticky Notes and Apple's Post-it, you can use to create some great-looking reminders you can place on several of your devices. Avoidance is another way to cut head clutter— sometimes. Avoiding certain elements of your job, when appropriate, can provide psychological benefits but might also gnaw away at your psychic energy. You can, for example, give yourself permission to mentally bundle up certain job-related details like a phone call you have to make or a meeting with administrators you want to steer clear of because a certain task requires it or because you lack the information you need for follow-through. You can put them in a mental safe, so to speak, lock the door, and permit yourself to open it at a more appropriate time. The beauty of this approach is that you get to tell yourself when that time will be most opportune for you, such as "I will call the applications office for results on the loan at four o'clock" or "I will speak with administrators about a new marketing strategy on Friday morning." The tipping point for using this approach is when dwelling or waiting induces more stress. So again, balance is key.

THE EMOTIONAL FACTOR

Regulating your emotions involves identifying what you do well under the influence of specific emotions and then arranging those activities for yourself. Like low energy and stressors, however, your emotions can also misguide your focus. As we've discussed, feeling depressed or blue can deplete your attention span and slow your memory. For instance, if you see the glass as half empty, so to speak, you may perceive details related to a potential work opportunity in a negative light; you may assume that they require too much effort for the prize or that they are rigged to benefit others rather than you. Such misperceptions often lead to unfavorable decisions and generate more stress and unhappiness. At times, we are all likely to feel depressed, angry, or fearful. However, during those times we can practice self-regulation by acknowledging these emotions and responding to them gainfully.

It's important to become aware of when a negative emotion has done its job so you can let it go. For example, let's say you experience fear about a potential health problem. Your adrenaline and cortisol spike enough to give you clarity on what to do next: make an appointment to see a doctor, where the problem can be addressed. Once you make the appointment, you can tell yourself that your fear has done its job by helping you get to where you need—the doctor's—and keeping it around any longer will only generate negative returns.

Sometimes you may even need emotions like feelings of situational depression to slow you down so you can rethink an important and imminent decision. The following scan will help you understand what an emotion is saying. Ask yourself these questions:

What am I feeling?
Is there an advantage in feeling this way at this particular moment in time?
What activities can I perform better in this state?

As an example, you may realize that when you're feeling emotionally lethargic, it is not an advantageous time to be making phone calls or conducting interviews. However, this may be the perfect state for you to analyze materials in your quiet space, because your critical skills are spiked when you are moving and thinking slower.

The concept of regulating emotions applies to positive emotions as well, because these can actually misguide your focus. When you're excited, for instance, you may become less critical and more likely to miss a strategic detail you would have otherwise caught. You may also be tempted to take on more work than you can handle. The best policy is to glance inwardly and keep yourself aware.

As mentioned, the idea is to match your emotions with activities you do best under their specific influence. That helps you meet tasks with a more positive mind-state and transfer that good feeling into your day in general. This strategy is also very helpful if you must work during a recovery from surgery, other health matters, or general rebounds.

Let me share an example from my own life. I tend to be a better reader (and listener) when I am in the doldrums, so I know that's a good time for me to reach for a book or an informational report. I can also lose myself effectively in analytical work when I'm down. In that way, taking care of the analytical business becomes my reward. Steeping myself in it then helps me shake off the blues, because my energy starts to get back into the flow. Losing yourself in a positive activity just for a little while might give you the quarter turn you need to get back on a more positive path. It will also help you stay there more easily.

TRY THIS!

Practice making yourself aware. List one positive work-related activity you do better when you are experiencing feelings of

- Situational depression
- Sadness
- Anger

LISTEN TO YOUR HORMONES

In addition to adrenaline and cortisol, your brain's other top-shelf attention influencers include dopamine, serotonin, and sex hormones. These hormones influence your moods as well as guide your attention to attach to certain details and away from others. This guidance is advantageous to some situations yet troublesome in others, so becoming sensitive to their subtle effects will help you control them to develop a stronger, more accurate attention span and, ultimately, selectivity. Let's take a look.

As with adrenaline, chemical shifts in body chemistry aren't always bad. For instance, research into the idea of the natural "highs" produced by exercise and other activities has become one of the most popular areas of brain study to this day. Today we know that scans of human brains during the release of self-produced, feel-good hormones during the anticipation or receipt of good news bear an uncanny resemblance to the brain scans of cocaine addicts. In fact, as you read this book, any of the chemicals washing over your brain at the moment are strong enough to require a license to prescribe. The important takeaway is that you can learn to regulate these chemical changes to reach sharper, more goal-appropriate states of mind. You can use them to stay on course naturally throughout the day with more energy, ease, and accuracy.

DOPAMINE

Dopamine is your brain's self-produced euphoric drug. It is associated (secreted) with rewarding behaviors. For instance, when you perceive that you have had a productive conversation with a prospective client, or you hear a piece of music you love, or you see a waiter carrying a tray with your dinner toward your table, you feel a rush of good vibes, and part of that rush is due to the dopamine released in your bloodstream. In terms of calming capability, dopamine is no joke; it is one of your strongest neurotransmitters. Dopamine production can be induced simply by thinking about or engaging in activities that give you pleasure—and everything leading up to them. Embedded in this process are the hormone's good and potentially harmful effects. Because of its ability to reward behaviors, dopamine plays a role in most addictive activity, so you have to watch out what you connect it to. Once you associate a behavior with pleasure, dopamine strengthens your motivations and the behavior as well. It would be easy, for instance, to make a detrimental behavior like tardiness a reward.

You can, however, control your dopamine pipeline by using any of several natural and positive methods, including guided imagery, natural sound, and music. Individually or combined, these tools can induce more of the hormone as well as keep it flowing longer. You can also learn to coordinate dopamine's release within specifically chosen goal-related situations—like calming your fears of asking for a coworker to participate on a joint project. One professional personality I know used music to diminish his fears of public speaking. He did this by placing an ethnic folk song his mother used to sing to him when he was a child on his cell phone and playing it randomly right up to the time he was to give the presentation. He said the song flooded him with great calming energy and comforting memories that produced just what he needed. With each application, the song worked its magic with stronger effect. Eventually his stress pattern naturally weakened and was replaced by the new, more calming, dopamine-spiced brain-wave pattern as a reward. This was exactly what he needed to strengthen his attentional beam. Singing, chanting, and humming can also be effective ways of releasing this brain drug and increasing attention span.

As a caution, when self-regulating your feelings of reward, don't overdo it. If you push your dopamine production too far, you can create an imbalance. Overproduction can deteriorate your focus. Too much dopamine will leave you unable to tell the difference between what is important and what isn't. This mind-set can chemically draw you toward risky behavior, so listening to what this hormone is saying is important in regulating yourself. Ask yourself if your focus is being enhanced or impaired. Make balance your goal, and remember that this means hitting your mind's sweet spot between calm and alert.

SEROTONIN

Serotonin is sometimes called your happy hormone. It is connected to better sleep and good moods, and can be increased with satisfying sleep, massage, and exercise.

Associated with balancing the effects of dopamine, serotonin also extends its influence to reaching higher-level thinking, reasoning, decision making, and goal-directed actions. Serotonin boosts empathy, so it helps you figure things out, especially when the content is emotional. If your dopamine levels are driving your focus toward detail that is extraneous to your goal, then serotonin can help keep you on track without losing sight of your target. If your emotional states are discombobulating, then balancing this hormone can help.

So, how do you increase the flow of serotonin? Fortunately, like dopamine, it also responds well to natural sound, music, and images, which you can use to bring your focus back on track when needed. Practicing higher awareness and self-regulation will reward your brain in your quest to find happiness, increasing your chances of success in the future, and it will keep you flowing.

SEX HORMONES

Most of us have encountered what I refer to as *Jekyll and Hyde moments* induced by high testosterone production. Testosterone is the sex hormone usually associated with men, but it is also produced by women in lesser amounts. The effects of hormonal shifts can feel very subtle to the person who is experiencing them. High-testosterone individuals, for instance, can suddenly and unknowingly become more aggressive with coworkers when they are assigned a task they feel is beneath them. Yet when the effects of the hormone wear off, they usually return to normal, often with no memory of what just happened. Of course, this hormone can also help workers pull a task together nicely, especially in demanding situations like last-minute assignments with tight deadlines that require a

fierce drive and determination to complete. Here, too, matching effects and goals is essential. In fact, becoming aware of the
peripheral effects of higher testosterone in your goal-related
attention can help smooth your interpersonal communications
and behaviors and lead to more satisfying workdays.

You can balance testosterone, sending production up or
down naturally, with exercise as well as with sound, music,
power words, and guided imagery. There are also many products available in today's market to boost your testosterone, but
you need to check with your physician to see which, if any, may
work for you.

Estrogen is the sex hormone associated with women, though
men do produce some estrogen, albeit in much smaller amounts
and apparently to no function. For women it has long been
known that estrogen provides an advantage in handling stress.
It sharpens memory and strengthens verbal communication.

Oxytocin, a hormone related to feelings of pleasure, also
seems to affect women more than men, adding a chemical
pushback to stressors and stress hormones. Oxytocin streams
through the blood rapidly during sexual climax, childbirth,
breast feeding, intimate touch, and massage. You can use the
same holistic tools discussed in this chapter to help stimulate
oxytocin production. Note that testosterone decreases oxytocin's capacity to help handle stressors, which is another reason
to balance that hormone.

Because all of these hormones can influence our behavior so
strongly, self-regulation is essential to controlling our destiny.
The alternative is zombie-like automatic perceptions, decisions,
and results. Know the peripheral signs of chemical thoughts and
feelings so you can use them to guide your thoughts and actions
toward your goals. With a little practice, you can gain control

over many more of life's important moments, day by day, week by week, and over your lifetime.

KNOW WHAT YOU BELIEVE

Like emotions and memories, what you believe can also influence where, how, and with what intensity you aim your attention. As well, it can affect what detail or information you choose to pay attention to and what you reject. Before you participate in an event or experience (or even during those moments), it is proactive to consider any preset beliefs you may have that you will carry into that experience and that may influence its outcome. You can do this through visualization prior to the event. Ask yourself, "Is there a belief I hold that is in conflict with thoughts and actions required to successfully pursue my goal?" Consider general social and cultural values you hold as well as personal beliefs about people, places, and procedures. Then ask yourself, "Is this my belief or someone else's? Do I still want hold on to this belief as I approach my goal? Is it connected to who I am today and who I want to be in the future? What thinking, emotional, and action patterns does it spark during my work-related experiences? How do I feel after? Does it make sense to continue to allow its influence in my workplace experiences? What steps can I take to reach that balance?"

Ultimately, your overall energy, the amount of stress you feel, your electrochemical activity, your emotions, and your beliefs all interact with each other to create your psychic currency and the quality of your attention span. Add the practices of balancing and cultivating energy to your daily routine, and keep flowing.

CHAPTER EXERCISES

Using Music to Alter Your Brain Waves

Music is able to alter your brain wave activity by slowing it down or speeding it up. In this way, music makes it possible for you to alter and create mental states (e.g., energized, focused, calm, or relaxed) without harmful side effects. When the BPM (beats per minute) is over 100, it will speed up brain waves, energizing you. For example, the Stray Cats' "Rock This Town" clocks in at 207 BPMs, while John Lennon's "Imagine" lands at 76. You can locate the BPM to your favorite songs by consulting songbpm. com or by googling BPM and going to any of the other available sites. You can also simply do a search for the song's title and BPM.

If you want to boost your energy, identify several favorite songs that you feel have an uplifting effect on you. Arrange them into a playlist you label "Energizing Playlist." You can arc your list going from lower to higher BPMs to energize yourself: e.g., 100, 110, 120, 130, 200. Alternately, if you want to increase your sense of calm, select songs that fit that category, label it accordingly, and arc them in reverse order. For best results, listen to your list for 7 minutes to energize and 12 minutes to calm.

Reversing Memory Fatigue

You can also use music to place your mind in a remembering mode that will enhance your recall when you need it. To do this, pick a song from as far back as you can remember, perhaps one you used to listen to with your mom or dad or one you listened to as a teen. Place yourself in a scene from the past by visualizing a mental narrative. Capture as much detail within your chosen scene as possible. Consider all your senses. I recommend playing the tune live on your cell phone or other device. However, you can alternately play it in your head. Enjoy your time travel for 10 to 12 minutes. If your song is shorter than 10–12 minutes, hit the repeat button or add more tunes as necessary. Then move on to your next activity.

Using a One-Minute Acupoint De-stressing Massage

This exercise shows you how to destress using a massage point called the *bubbling well,* which is located at the bottom center of each foot. From a seated position, locate the area at the bottom of either foot. Hold the foot with the opposite hand and gently massage the center area in circular motions with your thumb a few times. This exercise offers almost immediate stress release and leaves your energy in a balanced state of calm and alert.

8

What I Don't See Can't Hurt Me—Can It?

Rule #8

*Manage what you don't see if it has an
effect on your goals.*

Our minds often take the quickest, easiest way out in decision making. What's more, most of these choices happen at such lightning speed—just milliseconds—they don't feel like choices at all. You are suddenly just "there." Sometimes this leaves us uncompromising about decisions. You probably know coworkers, subordinates, managers, or clients who are generally close-minded. Those people probably have strong beliefs, affiliations, or track records that will slant them one way or another on particular subjects. One of the problems with this kind of closed thinking is that it is often self-reinforcing and can make people resistant to important information as it avails itself. But just how immobile is this state of mind really? Is simply being aware of it enough to make it a little less rigid, and does its rigidity necessarily mean it is incorrect or inaccurate? In light of the issues we've explored in previous chapters, here's another dilemma: how can we tell if we are truly making our own choices or if our mind is steering the ship in what *it* decides is the best direction, motivated by flight-or-fight impulses that don't fit the actual, present-day situation? These are all legitimate questions.

Consider this: Humans are pretty good at identifying faces. We can see faces everywhere—in swirls of paint, tie-dyed shirts, slabs of rock, and even in the bark of trees. Perhaps evolution gifted us with this capability to facilitate our social needs. In any case, we see them. As with other sensory details, we can convince ourselves that what we perceive is accurate. Why do we do it?

One reason is that we believe our convictions—and this can sometimes become challenging. Recently, researchers set up an experiment to see if they could convince people to defend a choice *they didn't even actually make.* Volunteers were shown two photos. They were asked to pick the photo of the person they identified as more attractive. Researchers, by sleight of hand, quickly switched the photo so that participants were now looking at the photo of a different person—actually the one they'd originally rejected. More than 80 percent of the participants didn't even notice the swap, transferring their conviction to the new photo instead and defended a choice they didn't even make. And in similar tests, participants became even further set in their manipulated preference the next time the choice was on the table.[1]

So, what does all this mean? It means that sometimes we make decisions that we think are totally in line with our personal objectives, but in fact they are completely opposite. Moreover, we can actually overlook and then forget the choice we'd actually prefer. How many of life's important decisions have we made like this? How many times have we rejected clues that hit us right in the face, indicating that employment choices, career choices, and relationships were not a good fit, yet we pursued them anyway?

Fortunately, you can improve your awareness, attention, and selection with self-monitoring. With practice, you will become more flexible, and you will discover that avoiding one-way thinking and opening new doors to freer, happier living is not as hard as it sounds.

As we've discussed throughout earlier chapters, we like to think we know our own minds, but that's just not always the case. Managers, teachers, parents—all of us—have initially defended decisions we later reconsidered. And because these decisions happen in just milliseconds, it can be hard to put on the brakes when we suspect we are veering off course. With some training, however, you can increase your odds of avoiding the screwup. Again, knowing a little of how your own mind operates and what your true goals are can help you choose and stay on the best path.

WHY DID I DO THAT? THAT ISN'T LIKE ME!

Choice blindness is a term used by psychologists to suggest that people aren't always aware of the choices they make. It refers to a phenomenon that causes people to be unable to accurately recall their choices. The concept of choice blindness can help explain how it is that you can get to places in your decision making that seem unreasonable or that seem out of character for you. Consider the experiment I referred to earlier in this chapter. Despite the fact that the pictures had been switched, participants continued to justify a choice they hadn't even made, with statements such as "I liked the earrings" or "I liked the hairstyle" *when they had not made these selections at all.* The researchers found that people also stuck with their "decision" (again, one they only *believed* they had made) by exhibiting the same lack of awareness and the same willingness to validate manipulated choices when their actions involved senses like taste, or even moral decisions.[2] Generally, people like to justify their choices, whether those decisions reflect the way they really feel or not. At risk is that we can fail to identify whether an action is authentic. To complicate things, we can end up assuming ownership of thoughts, feelings, and actions that have been manipulated under our radar. As such, we may not know our real choices as well as we think we do.

HOW LONG HAS THAT BEEN STARING ME IN THE FACE?

Ever drive down a street, see a certain building you've never noticed, and wonder, "Wait a minute. Has that always been there?" Later you discover it has been under construction for months and now it's finished. You have driven by it many times during its construction, but you somehow missed the whole process and completion. This phenomenon is known as *change blindness,* the inability to notice changes in a scene. You can find examples of change blindness in many film and television shows that include errors missed by the editors. My children love to make a game of seeing if they can find these inconsistencies. Just the other night, for example, we were watching a mystery set in an old New England house. One of the room's windows showed that it was raining hard outside, yet when the camera panned to a different window in the same room, there was no rain in the scene at all.

Change blindness can affect our gut feelings, which can slant our attention. For example, we tend to dismiss information that we may see as against our "tribe" or our beliefs. Hence we reject corporate, political, cultural, departmental, and regional information that we feel cuts against theories or ways of thinking that are important to us. Yet this can actually prevent us from making good choices. Whenever you are tempted to dismiss an offer automatically, you should consider these potentially harmful tendencies and ask yourself, "What am I dismissing here? And why?" This approach can often get you on track.

TRY THIS!

The next time you look at a sales flier ask yourself, "Why am I attracted to a certain word or image over another? What inferences can I make about my emotions, memory, and beliefs and how they may be guiding my focus?" We tend to base our thoughts and actions on the way we have done things before, giving these links preference. Consequently, if you don't update—and sometimes change—your beliefs, memories, and procedures, you will find it hard to regulate an upcoming choice. Instead, the act of relying on old patterns makes you blind to details and sets you up to keep doing things the same way.

To prevent choice blindness in one situation from affecting your behaviors and thinking further down the road, step back once in a while to extend your sights. For example, let's say you need to make a decision about which person to use for an upcoming job. Instead of going with your automatic choice, step back and ask yourself, "How might that decision affect the bigger picture? How might it affect myself, my coworkers, and the organization next week, next month, or next year?"

Let's say that after the fact, the motivations for and the results of your decision become clearer. From that vantage point, take time to ask yourself, "Which influencers do I want to keep active the next time I am in a similar situation? Which do I want to dismiss?" This can help you imprint a pattern for change that you can implement in the future.

INATTENTIONAL BLINDNESS

Mix-ups happen in all situations. A college professor about to teach a class for the first time enters a room with the right number...in the wrong building. An auto mechanic who expects that her partner put the oil cap back in place returns the car to its owner and then it catches fire on the highway. (This actually happened to my friend's vehicle.) Serious errors even occur in the medical world with the administration of a wrong drug or dosage or a missing reference to a drug allergy in a prescription. To err is human, it's true, but we can all get better at minimizing our chances of making mistakes, particularly in higher-risk situations.

Part of the problem is that just because information enters your field of vision doesn't mean that you've "seen" it. You need to focus on it. In fact, as we have been saying, our brains are taking in a massive amount of information as we approach any task, and we can only pay attention to a very small amount of it. Some of the left-out information can turn out to be important to our decisions, and so we err. Sometimes, as with the professor, the error is literally the size of a building! And sometimes the damage is that big. How do we miss it?

The phenomenon is known as *inattentional blindness*, a

term coined by Dr. Arien Mack, New School of Social Research, and Dr. Irvin Rock, University of California, in the late 1990s. Connected to change blindness, it is associated with focusing on one thing that may cause you to lose focus on another. For example, as you focus on reading email on your cell phone, you fail to see an unexpected pothole and trip. Or as you are focused on an employee's bold outfit, you fail to see his genius social skills.

The concept of inattentional blindness was captured by one of the most well-known psychological experiments of all time, the "invisible gorilla" experiment. For the experiment, participants watch a short video where a team of three people in black shirts are passing a basketball back and forth with three people in white shirts. Participants are instructed to count how many times the team in white shirts passes the ball. After a little bit, a gorilla walks through the game, stands in the middle, and hammers its chest. Then it leaves the scene. Next, participants are asked if they saw the gorilla. "More than half the time, people miss the gorilla entirely. More than that, even after the participants are told about the gorilla, they're certain they couldn't have missed it.[3] The takeaway? Because you primarily focus on what you expect in an event, you can totally miss an unexpected yet huge detail.

To anticipate attentional blindness in your own life, consider where your activity requires you to aim your focus. If you are looking for a certain type of restaurant, for instance, it is easy to miss seeing traffic signs as you peruse the streets. If you are reading a menu, you can miss seeing a client seated across from you. Conversely, if you overuse attentional cues, like highlighting too many passages in a text, those passages may begin to lose their contrast and no longer stand out enough. The same effect can occur with color coding.

Flexibility helps. Remember the formula from chapter 4: Think as you go from one task to another: focus/execute/rinse/repeat. Use it often, and don't forget to rinse. So, be sure to clear your head between tasks. This approach will help keep your focus flexible, and it will help you push back at inattentional blindness.

Reflection also helps. Looking back over your actions in an event in which you missed information can make you privy to what factors may have driven your focus off target—such as you answered a customer's random question just as you began to fill her order and you put the wrong product in her bag. You can, with practice, slow down your tendency to repeat a similar action. For instance, reflecting on an alternative action to help keep you focused—such as telling the customer what you are doing and naming the product you are placing in her bag—can help activate your preferred response.

WHOSE BRAIN LOVES SHORTCUTS?

Everyone's brain loves shortcuts. The term *cognitive miser* was coined in the mid-1980s by Dr. Susan Fiske, professor of psychology at UCLA, and Dr. Shelley Taylor, distinguished professor emeritus of psychology also at UCLA. The *miser brain* describes your brain's tendency to want to be a cognitive miser, to problem-solve quickly, relying on shortcuts to use the least mental effort and bypassing your thinking process. So for a multitude of reasons—including times when you are feeling low energy, don't want to think too much, or don't want to rattle your emotions or another person's emotions—your decisions are apt to take the quickest, easiest trail. This comes at a cost. For one, fast-tracked decisions calculated by your brain's miser mode can also cause you to miss relevant information, focus on the wrong things, and proceed to disadvantageous actions. Take, for instance, a person driven by the desire for promotion. Miser brain can propel her to accept an unrealistic time frame to complete a project she believes will help her achieve her goal. A person who is driven by the need to appear as a team player may keep silent when several members of his team are superenthusiastic about an upcoming marketing plan, despite the fact that he sees flaws in their strategy.

The larger problem in these cases is that once you chemically connect a miser state to your brain's reward system (dopamine), it becomes further ingrained and harder to change. As such, miser brain can affect your reasoning. Instead of working each step toward solutions logically, you'll find that it's easy to replace reason, out of convenience, with more automatic responses often guided by desire, emotion, beliefs, or feelings of reward and former ways of doing things. If you are excited over the possibilities of a new business agreement, for example, you may tend toward attaching to information that will make things look sweeter and overlook the crunch details needed to get it on the road, so to speak. Whereas your brain's miser system might help you negotiate a left-hand turn at a traffic light, it can at times prevent you from getting a full perspective on decisions.

Let's say you're interviewing someone for a job. Your miser brain wants to take the shortcut of identifying a potential problem—whether it is genuine or not—to help you quickly make up your mind. For instance, the miser brain might raise your ingrained misgivings about people with tattoos, conflating the applicant's tattoos with poor job performance. However, if you can become aware of what your mind is doing, then you can release old beliefs and see the candidate fully. In all situations, it's important to recognize that your former gut feelings may be inaccurate. Then you can generate more open links and thought processes and, in this example, incorporate them into part of your hiring methods in the future.

Harvard Business Review suggests that a bit of uncertainty can help you control your brain's miser because it can make you think twice and come to better decisions.[4] Whenever you find that you are eager to cut to the chase during decision making, avoid errors by considering three possibilities: a worst-case scenario, a medium-case scenario, and a best-case scenario. To ensure you are making a solid decision and not jumping the gun, it is usually safe to choose the medium-case scenario. Go with the average.

I also read the term *premortem* in the *Harvard Business Review,* and I loved it. The term emphasizes that we can stomp out a bad pathway before it gets legs. Premortem is a specific visualization in which you imagine what details might cause a certain upcoming decision or project to fail. This gives you the opportunity to address problems before they occur and apply corrective measures. Having access to these details in memory as a preset helps you better navigate through the developing scenario in real time.[5] This approach is absolutely spot on.

Stay flexible. Consider it a way to push back against your miser brain. Give yourself some leeway to consider your options. Here are some questions you can ask yourself when facing a decision.

What skills or perceptions do not come naturally in an important upcoming situation?

Which should I pay attention to?

What details am I vulnerable to in this current situation that may make me miserly in decisions?

Adding these kinds of questions to your processing approach will leave you less vulnerable to errors. Practice will generate the pause you need to consider broader options. Allowing yourself other options—even opposite ones—can free you. Then, after making a decision, reflect your way through it in reverse. This step will help you become aware of what occurred in your head; it will help you better understand and learn from what took place; and it will allow you to update the links in your memory for future behavior.

Building on our discussion in chapter 7, your psychic energy affects not only your focus but also your mind's tendency to get miserly. The more you fatigue, the more your mind skips to solutions. You give up deeper thinking and learning. So, as a check, ask yourself, "What may I be losing out on by taking the fast track?" On a personal level, I recently did this with a contract and wound up with a much more attractive package, so I highly recommend fighting off the urge to quickly dot the proverbial "Is" and cross the "Ts." Even if your new choice requires you to cultivate more energy than the shortcut would have entailed, the exercise and tools throughout this book can help you out.

PRIMES

Ever head into a shop for the first time and suddenly feel fantastic? What about heading into an office and feeling like the life is being sucked out of you? Or maybe you're walking down the cookie aisle in your grocery store and next thing you know you are buying not only cookies but also the whole nine yards—the cocoa and milk as well—even though none of these items were on your list. Such effects are often the result of what psychologists call *priming*.

Priming is an unconscious connection to external stimuli (words, images, sounds, and so on), memory, and experiences. It occurs when exposure to certain details activates your responses due to your prior experiences. Priming works on you just like a remote control and it happens under your radar. Further, primed behaviors increase the likeliness of other responses linked to them in your memory. So primes trigger behaviors by association. For example, in chapter 1, we saw how a list of white objects might trigger you to quickly pick *milk* in response to the question, "What do cows drink for breakfast?" Similarly, if you have recently responded to a word like *pharmacist* in a random list of words, you are more likely to pull the word *drug* out of a string of random letters afterward. On the other hand, when you intentionally choose to ignore specific stimuli, you respond more slowly when those details come up again. So if as I am checking in customers I specifically ignore the waiting room television when it's on, it has less effect the next time it enters my awareness. Or if I regularly ignore a sign that says "Emergency Procedures," I am likely to become better at disregarding it. This effect is known as *negative priming*. It's effective when you are trying to inhibit or eliminate certain details from your focus—as with interruptions. Yet you have to be careful what you ignore, because each time you do so, you are making it more difficult to catch the next time.

"Pretty much everything can be primed," said John Bargh, a social psychologist currently working at Yale University. Mention the word *library* and people tend to speak more quietly. Put a photo of a loved one on your desk and you start behaving as if that person was physically with you. Carry a briefcase and people may compete with you.[6] According to Bargh, "We are faced with an embarrassment of riches with all these effects. Our task now is to try and make sense of them."[7]

All of this may make you think twice before putting a new

painting on the wall in your office or picking a certain news item to read right before, say, a crucial interview, an essential work task, or an important event. But just how powerful can primes be?

Dr. Christian Wheeler, a professor and honored scholar at Stanford University, has conducted numerous compelling experiments on how much influence objects can have on people. One such experiment was his briefcase study. In the "business objects" condition, Wheeler took questionnaires out of a black briefcase; asked participants to complete these surveys with a silver-barreled, executive-style pen; and then instructed them to put the completed surveys into a black executive portfolio. Then he repeated the experiment with a different set of participants, taking the questionnaires out of a black backpack, asking participants to use pencils, and instructing them to place the surveys in a cardboard box when finished. This was considered the "neutral objects" condition.

His goal was to determine if the business objects (i.e., the pens, pencils, backpack, briefcase, etc.) would influence participants to hold on to more money in an *ultimatum game* (a game commonly used in economics) in which participants believed they were in a position to receive some money and would have to propose a way to divide that money between themselves and another individual. As it turned out, the objects did. On the other hand, those in the neutral objects group turned out to be less greedy.[8] Another part of the same study showed that people perceived an ambiguous scenario as more competitive once they'd been exposed to the business objects.[9]

Such unconscious influences shape the way we think, feel, and act daily. They can prime how we feel about ourselves and others, and anything in your environment can become a trigger. However, just because you are unaware, this doesn't mean you must remain unaware. You could, for instance, use reflection to become sensitive to objects that can have an influence on you. You can learn to recognize cues and make useful conclusions such as these: "When I stay interested in a project, the outcome is usually successful" or "Before my meeting, I thought of something nice I'd do with my family over the weekend, and the meeting went more amiably than usual." Alternately, you might recognize the opposite: "I talked profusely about my associate's stubbornness before our business lunch, and it impinged on my ability to get through to him when I needed to."

In this way, you can try to eliminate a prime's further influence on you. As well, awareness through reflection on everyday sights, sounds, smells, and encounters can help you identify and utilize positive primes that you feel facilitate your goals, and it can help you eliminate disruptive primes. Once you develop a sense of particular influencers, you can surround yourself with environments that promote your goals. For instance, if you are trying to become a better listener, then surround yourself with examples from certain films, literature, poems, songs, images, and affirmations.

So much of what you don't see can have a profound effect on your thinking, feelings, and goals. How you respond (or not) will create new links that will trigger your future behaviors. So consider alternate solutions that will challenge your first thoughts regarding workday tasks. Remember that just because you are unconscious to many of the networks affecting your choices, you don't have to remain unaware.

CHAPTER EXERCISES

Expanding Your Options

As this chapter has shown, your previous beliefs link their influence to your current goals. As you approach a goal, ask yourself if your former perceptions and actions toward similar goals still make sense. By neutralizing these convictions altogether, you can sometimes grant yourself a wider lens on potentially good (sometimes better) solutions. It can also help you clarify risks in your strategy. A quick, mindful scan is all it will take. Ask yourself, "What if I took an alternate or even opposite position? How would that change my strategy and results? What would I say if I were giving advice to someone else about this situation?" Examining your mental links will help you activate the ones you find functional and inhibit those you do not.

Scheduling a New Initiative

As Warren Buffett has said, "Should you find yourself in a chronically leaking boat, energy devoted to changing vessels is likely to be more productive than energy devoted to patching leaks."[10] Often if you stay with a strategy long enough, it gets harder to get unstuck when it's not working out, yet your mind defers to it over and over. To combat this, establish a date when you will kick an alternate plan into action. Tell yourself, "If things don't change I will start a new training program starting _____." Pick a date and use it as your checkpoint. Make flexibility part of the plan. Prepare, in advance, more than one strategy that is capable of hitting your goal. Tweak any aspects of the initial strategy as you progress toward your checkpoint. If you reach the checkpoint and realize that your plan is not working, consider your new initiative.

Cuing Options to a Preset

Novice decisions can throw you off, so it can help to have a list of considered options cued to a preset. Cue yourself as follows: "If this _____ happens and I mess up, then I will do this _____."

Using Beginner's Mind

Next time you engage in an activity place yourself in a state of *Beginner's Mind*. A concept in Asian traditions, Beginner's Mind is the mind-set with which you approach a task fully conscious and alert, with absolutely no negative preconceptions. You approach it as if you are going to a job you've wanted for a long time and now you have it. Beginner's Mind frees you of habits of experience and helps you see things as they are. It helps keep you full of positive energy, excited, and open.

9

Wide and Narrow
Vision Are Partners

Rule #9

*Know when to concentrate your attention vs.
when to open it wide.*

You shift your focus from broad to narrow and back again constantly throughout the day. Think of it as adjusting a camera lens back and forth. You can peer at an entire baseball team positioned across the field, or you can tighten up and choose to zero in on just one player. You utilize the function whenever you scroll on your word processing screen to locate a specific print font and size, select it and then check out how it looks in your document. Knowing when to concentrate or open your focus effectively isn't a question of putting this function to work more often. Rather, it's about consciously shifting when it will make a difference.

The concept of broadening and narrowing your focus is not just about zeroing in on objects strewn across a table, so to speak. It is also at the very heart of almost any creative endeavor. You might begin by looking at the wide array of information bubbling up around a project—a concept from a lecture, a thought, a feeling, and so on—and then peering in more narrowly on details you suddenly find interesting. You may be looking for a new, exciting angle with which to connect information to a current goal. Or you may be looking for a unique goal that can be constructed from unfamiliar or familiar details.

Journalism classes offer a good example of how this works. A popular exercise asks students to review a series of facts and details about an event and then write the story. Students are all working with the same details but still need to organize them. What should they lead with, end with, and emphasize? How are they going to assemble the details? They also need to decide what tones to use, which definitions to supply, and the point readers must arrive at—such as an explanation, a prediction, or a word of caution. It's up to each writer to see a twist to construct from the details, and so forth. The idea is that creativity comes from what each person does with the facts and the way each writer sees them.

So your attention is continuously shifting back and forth. Like observing a picture that is developing within your mind, you watch as each piece creates and affects the whole—until you think you've got it the way you want it.

This shifting technique works with all sensory, cognitive, and emotional information. Imagine listening to an orchestra that has 100 players. For the majority of the time, you are focused on listening to the whole wave of music coming at you. However, you know that whenever you want, you can focus on just the cellos or the percussion or any single section of the orchestra. And you could at any moment reassemble all the pieces into a unified broader sound with a better appreciation of how the cellos or percussion instruments contribute to the whole.[1]

What's more, you can preset this mechanism. As such, you

can have it ready to go when you need it. By broadening and narrowing your focus on a text, idea, image, sound, or other sensory information, you can put the mode in the ready position for your next task. For example, if you practice in advance of reviewing notes for a project or preparing for a professional meeting, taking a test, or the like, then the mind-set follows you. This allows you to alternate more gracefully (and automatically) from a wide to narrow purview in your next activity. This is a great technique to preset. As more examples, it will help public speakers to zero in on answers to questions at events, teachers to detail answers for students, and test takers to recall specific facts on an exam.

As we've discussed in earlier chapters, from the perspective of holistic psychology and mind-body medicine, I favor using sound as a way of transferring and transforming a variety of mind-states, including this one. Using your favorite music—be it orchestral or rock or any style—is an easy way to start your mind shifting between a concentrated and open focus. All you have to do is play your selected tune, narrowing your focus to one instrument throughout or to a repeating vocal line or guitar riff. Then wait for it to come around again. For this approach to work, you need to use an element you like a lot. You can then play back the tune with anticipation and pull back your focus, paying attention to how your segment enhances the entire piece.

Fulfillment of your expectations ties the listening process to your body's reward hormones, including dopamine and serotonin. This will more deeply ingrain your flowing mind-state and generate higher-level thinking as you shift between widening and narrowing your spotlight. Regular practice makes the process more and more fluid and automatic. The nice thing about using music is that it's convenient. You can simply put songs on your cell phone, save them in a file with a title like "Wide & Narrow Focus Training," and carry the mind-set in your pocket. You can then have it at the push of a button whenever you need it.

DON'T BE CUELESS

Soccer and other sports provide more good examples of the need to navigate from broad to narrow vision. Sometimes you must do so in split seconds. Soccer experts maintain that a player, for example, may need to keep a broad focus as she dribbles the ball downfield in order to keep an eye on teammates and opponents and yet simultaneously evaluate her next potential actions. However, once she decides to either take a shot or serve the ball into the box, she may need to narrow her focus on the exact target, such as the goal or her teammate. Using the higher energy of mindfulness and keeping the gist information in her awareness makes this work with precision. In a way she is scoping the field like a dragonfly, compiling two paths of action simultaneously and then selecting and executing her move swiftly and decisively.

In soccer, this zoom-lens focus is continuous in order to make successful decisions and actions in all areas of the game. Other sports, in contrast, require players to hold more of a narrow focus. Sports like swimming and diving rely on a tighter spotlight because their environments do not change greatly, and athletes focus more on their own body and overall energy management. For soccer and tennis, where the environment is constantly changing, athletes need to sway from broad or narrow focus, depending on the emerging situation.[2]

In sports, making yourself aware of the circumstances in which you need a specific type of focus (wide vs. narrow) is a good first step to improvement through regulation and training. After that, getting yourself to the point where you are able to shift back and forth automatically comes out of your practice.

In the sports world if you can't shift between a narrow and broad focus you may wind up chasing a decoy and missing opportunity. Similarly, workers can get duped into a bad decision or conflict by an erroneous detail they narrowly focus on and attach to, such as deciding to work a late shift because daytime tasks have been made to look more tedious.

Whether in sports or the workplace, using cues to help you shift your focus when it strays is a surefire way to fine-tune the mechanism. If you notice your mind wandering during a task or decision, you can use a cue like "zero in, zero in" and instantly tighten your focus. Or you can broaden your focus, "widen your lens, widen your lens."

DON'T OVERDO IT

Evolution packed us with automatic presets. Finding food, running away, and fighting are three examples. These are rooted in the internal information we all carry in our head. And, as we have been saying, you can willfully generate your own. When you mentally rehearse actions—which can range from completing a golf stroke to dealing with a suddenly emotional colleague—your brain wires the behavior a little more tightly for the next time.[3] Your response time quickens, and your actions hit closer to what you want.

There is an energy cost, however, in learning the algorithms, as well as in training them. The cost involves the time spent figuring them out and putting them in place. The process, though, is well worth the expense. Here's an example.

Someone unexpectedly asks for your opinion at an organizational meeting. Pausing is not your usual habit, yet you accidentally do. Within that moment, you broaden your lens, you consider the wider range of how your answer will affect the organization and your coworkers as well as any immediate goals. Then you zero in, pick your answer carefully, and respond more advantageously than usual. Later, through reflection, you can make yourself aware of the difference your behavior (in this case, pausing) made. You can learn to create top-down cues based on your reflections so you can preset and repeat a good response in the future. This helps you build more confidence in your responsiveness to emergent situations. You feel better about the results.

At the same time, take care not to overthink things. When you do, you'll give too much control to circuits that know how to think and worry but not how to deliver the move you need.[4] Generally, overloaded attention (thinking too much) will cause you to choke—such as when you try to remember your own phone number, a person's name, or your child's birthday; during those times you clearly know it like the back of your hand but you just can't find it in your head. However, once you relax and open your focus wide, suddenly you can recall the information immediately. Overloading chokes your ability to self-regulate, so balance is best.

TRAINING

Training your mind to automatically shift back and forth from its wide to narrow focusing lens involves a process of guidance, selection, and enhancement. The guidance and selection elements begin with making yourself preaware of significant goals and enhancing them with word cues. Turning again to soccer as an example, players can use task prompts as triggers. These help manage what players need to be thinking and when and where players need to be guiding their focus. For instance, soccer players can teach themselves to zoom in or out using prompts like *ball* or *shot, shot.*

Whether you are an athlete or not, the idea is the same. You create cues appropriate to your task beforehand. This way, you establish some guidance and selectivity in advance. Remember, performance-related cues are doubly effective in that while activating your focus to important details, they will also inhibit irrelevancies.

Sometimes problematic situations are brewing under your radar. Consider this scenario: Sam is the director of a pharmaceutical research lab. Most of his coworkers consider him congenial, but some do not. He is aware of a frictional undercurrent with those individuals, but his fix is to be what he considers even more hospitable and lighthearted at times. For instance, he deepens his voice and claps male technicians on the back as he talks about their contribution to the organization's most recent grant approval, while at the same time he thanks the "ladies" (his choice word), who are also technicians, for their hard work on the grant proposal. Because of his deliberately assumed tone, Sam believes he's giving off nothing but congenial signals. He's being lighthearted, right? However, in reality his language choices are spurring an undercurrent of problems. When certain employees don't connect with him on his next project, he feels befuddled.

In addition to word cues, you can use social and cultural details to better engage goal-related action. Sam's use of language is causing him issues at the workplace. If he is to regulate it, he has to widen his lens to see how it is affecting employees and then tighten his focus, putting himself in their shoes, to see what language he uses that upsets them. Ultimately, meaning and effectiveness is in the hands of your audience. You'll get nowhere if you spark resistance in colleagues or clients because of a lackadaisically chosen word or reference. It can be as obvious as flubbing up the pronunciation of an individual's name or as subtle as using titles like *dean, colonel, nurse, professor,* or *pops* when you regard individuals of a certain culture, race, gender identification, organization, age, and so forth. This kind of discriminating communication may be under your radar as the speaker, but it won't be under the radar of your listeners.

The same is true when you voice common generalizations like "All progressives are extremists" or "All conservatives resist change." Unfortunately, there are a ton more, including "All radical approaches are dangerous." "All lawyers are interested in is money." "All musicians are hipsters." The list goes on and on. Such misguided language choices also includes the use of insensitive humor with disturbing implications to various individuals and groups. Feelings of disrespect are prime causes of interpersonal conflict and botched goals.

There is an answer close by. Visualizations and reflections to help you preset and update more inviting and successful social verbiage can expose your areas of vulnerability. It really doesn't take much, just looking closely at the situation and taking into consideration others' professional, social, and cultural backgrounds. The nice thing about language is, like various seasonings, you can spice things up differently—and still appropriately—per audience.

Most of your day is spent relying on a wide-lens, bottom-up flow of data. Things are mostly just happening and you are doing, not thinking about it. Yet it's hard to think that to some extent, you don't rely on both emerging detail and stored cues to get the job done. It's really a joint guidance/selection system. For instance, you make a pot of coffee. You put the filter and water in your coffeemaker, scoop out the coffee, place it in the receptacle, and you're ready to go. But at some point you had to know where the coffee and filters were located (top-down).[5]

Many times your processing of emerging (bottom-up) information is loaded with lessons. Nevertheless, as in Sam's story, you are not necessarily aware. You do something one way. You think it is working; perhaps your action could be better, you think, but as far as you know, you're getting by. At the beginning of this book, we referred to this thinking as sufficing. And it is endemic. By now you can see that the biggest contributor to a mind-set that settles for mediocrity is drone-like, inattentive living. But the other option is: self-regulation.

Your attentional links constantly update. You can enhance the process by consciously regulating upgrades for daily situations you want to control better. Lessons then link up to become top-down cues for future actions—e.g., you can't find your coffee scoop where you just put it and you remember (a cue) that last time this happened you'd placed it in its "old" cupboard space; you look and there it is. You notice, by narrowing your focus in a reflection, there is a look of disappointment on an employee when you refer to her as one of the "ladies" but to another employee as Dr. Rob. You notice that specific changes in work scheduling kept your workday on target when computers were "down." So learning is key—whether it is in real time or in reflection. In fact, learning itself will eventually become automatic. Just make sure you are learning the right thing. You can, for example, unconsciously be teaching yourself, by repeating a certain behavioral pattern, to work against your goals, to achieve less, and to accrue less satisfaction. You can "learn" and update better ways to anger, get disappointed, and stop reaching for your dream. You can begin to think that your situation is just the way it has to be. But in fact it can be just the opposite. Reflection after important experiences is essential. It is a great way to become more aware of when zooming in or out on detail is either enhancing or hindering your goals and your harmony around the workplace. I recommend using this tool often.

COLOR ZOOM CUES

Color and spatial cues can trigger strategic shifts from broad to narrow attentional lenses. Such cues are another type *top-down biasing.* Say you are trying to lower your cholesterol. You can use a mantra like "eat green" to remind you those foods are good when you go out to restaurants.[6] You can use the colors of traffic lights. Yellow, for example can cue you into widening lens in order to consider more information in certain moments. You can use red for when to put the brakes on completely and abort mission. And green for when to narrow your focus, zero in on your target, and execute. Possibilities are endless. I encourage you to create your own.

THE FAST YET INCREMENTAL APPROACH

In the *Harvard Business Review,* writers Thomas Hout and David Michael highlighted certain business concepts that they believe drive Chinese companies. These, they feel, are somewhat different in formula from those concepts that are steering Westerners. The signature model for Chinese companies, as I see it, is to create, put your creation out there (or into action), get feedback, adapt to feedback, and speedily put it out there again—continuing the feedback loop.[7] It places emphasis on speed and turnover.

To accomplish this, there is a constant widening and narrowing of focus. It starts with drilling out the concept. Historically, in Chinese philosophy this is accomplished with a wide-angle focus—the scattering of many seeds (not just one), so to speak, to see which ones take root. Once the best concept (or product/goal) emerges from these, a launch strategy is generated, then engaged, and afterward assessed. Then your perspective narrows as you edit for changes and updates and then loop through the process again. The formula is very different from Western strategizing, where we try something out and want it to last. And speed is not always our major factor.

Hout and Michael believe that Chinese companies offer some good lessons that are applicable to the workplace. These lessons include the simultaneous juggling of several concerns, such as organization, new information, and independence. The element of speed is strategized into their model to help you gain the most from your endeavors. In this plan, you de-emphasize a "stay with it for the long term" outlook, which allows you to hit goals and improve on them in less time. Then, going on to your next step with improvements, continuing your forward movement becomes more important than staying there for the long haul. You accelerate goal achievement but also include careful examination and reorganization. In theory, at least, you wind up ahead.

Individuals need to feel incremental, steady, and effective rewards that line their wallets and feed their passions. In this way, the Chinese model is something to be considered, but it doesn't have to be applied only to marketing. Each of us, in a sense, is our own product. You can guide your own workplace and career development by placing your attention on incremental change. For instance, you might decide to get an online degree, going as fast as the granting institution will allow, accruing as many transferable and life-experience credits as possible, reassessing with advisers at various markers (e.g., course completions, credits completed, and so on) to deepen and help speed you through the process. Then upon completing the program, now retrained, you could widen your lens in a new direction. You might try scattering many seeds for potentially better, more satisfying employment, including factors like apprenticeships and so on that will head you toward the growth you desire. Along the way, you could continue to widen your lens, scatter your ideas, see which ones take root, pursue them with speed and flexibility, reexamine and edit them as needed (while in pursuit and after), and thus set up the best deal for yourself!

Practice widening and narrowing your attention for tasks. Make some daily effort to reflect on the particulars of today as well as consider where you want to be tomorrow, next week, next month, next year, and five years from now, with a plan to incrementally double your vocational collateral.

CHAPTER EXERCISES

Using Cue Enhancement

Teach yourself to zoom in or out on detail by using a guidance, selection, and enhancement cue. I recommend establishing this technique as a preset. Here's how.

1. Review your goal in your mind.
2. Visualize yourself in the activity you want to regulate.
3. Locate spots where your concentration starts to bottle-neck in the activity (e.g., when you have been concentrated on one element too long).
4. Generate a word cue, similar to the soccer players in this chapter, such as "ease up" or "pull back."
5. Use these cues to guide your mind's eye into a wider view of detail.
6. Next, create a zeroing-in cue to narrow your focus, such as "that's it" or "yeah" as you spot and select the right detail.

With practice your mind will begin moving back and forth more smoothly. Remember, cues enhance your attention by activating your focus on important details and inhibiting irrelevancies. Apply cue enhancement in real-time performance.

Using Visualization as a Preset

You can use this technique in a vast assortment of situations. For this exercise, let's consider your word selection and body language the next time you assign or accept work.

1. At some point beforehand, visualize your personal and mutual goals in the situation.
2. Next, visualize yourself in the scene and observe the details playing out in your mind. See how your words and body language affect the others. Note their words and body language. Note their responses to your actions.
3. Step back in your visualization, making your focus wider. Ask yourself, "What should I encourage in terms of my chosen words and body language within my approach? What should I discourage?"
4. Play the scenario again with that approach in mind, and edit where necessary.
5. Establish cues to guide your selected word choices at crucial points in the imagined scenario (e.g., "compliment now" or "welcome" or "honey on your tongue" or "slow down").

10

I Know You; You Know Me

Rule #10

Remember the Golden Rule.

Empathy is a major circuit for regulating high-quality attention. Researchers have known for years that people who are more empathetic are more successful at work and in their personal lives. Beyond behavioral sciences, nearly every spiritual tradition on earth also teaches that your ability to empathize helps you establish happy, peaceful, and successful actions wherever you go. So what elements of this circuit do we rely on so much? What's going on in our head when empathy is working properly? And what happens when it's not? Can we actually learn empathy?

For now, let's define empathy as letting other people's feelings into your attention. This allows you to be able to consider—and learn—how your behavior affects them. Understanding others from this vantage point assists you in predicting how others may respond to your actions, and it exposes consequences as you work toward daily goals. Empathy in part is the result of a mirroring effect in your mind. This capacity is able to deliver a gauge between your Self and those around you and mutual goals. It allows you to identify details that promote harmony and unity with others.

What happens when you lack empathy? Take, for example, a nonempathetic person who creates a plan to better serve his customers. However, while his plan gets *him* what he wants, it puts his team and company at risk. His plan isn't much good in that case. Fortunately, things don't have to go this way. If you take the time to connect with others around you—examining the mirror images in your head to identify how your own thoughts, actions, and feelings contribute (or not) to the way things are turning out in the bigger picture—you can go forward with, fine-tune, or terminate your approach as needed.

Whether you are working with individuals or organizations, you will truly benefit from this approach. When you put in the time to connect, you are better able to pair your own goal-related needs with the needs of others. Because it helps harmonize your feelings about yourself with your actions, empathy has a lot to do with feeling real, self-confident, and appreciated. All of this snowballs into a stronger self-core from which you can progress toward your goals. You become more adept at generating win-win experiences. As such, empathy has a rippling effect. Use these circuits. Empathy improves everything you do.

THE COOL, WARM, AND HOT OF INFORMATION

You may notice that information you put your sights on carries inside it an inherent emotionality. Attention allows you to toggle among hot, warm, and cool emotional content. Emotional intelligence, on the other hand, characterizes your ability to decipher these as well as to respond to them in harmony with others and goals.[1] Your empathic system helps make effective adjustments as you go along. In this way, the systems of attention, emotional intelligence, and empathy are related. Let's consider this more closely.

Hot information refers to personally reported details that have personal importance, *cool information* exists on the other end of that spectrum, and *warm information* falls in between. For example, from cool to hot, I can say, "The Berkshires are on the East Coast" (cool information); "My wife and I live in the Berkshires (warm information); "I love my wife" (hot information). Emotional intelligence involves toggling among all three types to achieve the best result in any situation.

Let's say you need to decide whether to place a photo of two birds eating out of a bird feeder or two birds mating in your living room. Cool information just won't work. And simply paying attention to just the hot or cold details is more a naïve focus than an intelligent one. This applies from considering your reaction to a disgruntled customer to a discussion with your boss over a promotion to what paintings or art you decide to place on your office walls. You'll eventually have to involve your empathy machinery.

Daniel Goleman, in his book *Emotional Intelligence*, makes the case that men who practice emotional intelligence demonstrate more social grace, experience more balance, and are not so much swayed by fears or worries. They are more relaxed with themselves and their social environments. Women who show emotionally intelligent strength tend to be more assertive, feel more positive, and believe that their life is purposeful.[2] Consciously selecting how best to move forward in a situation by using empathy to consider its cool, warm, or hot informational makeup will help you leverage goals to your advantage throughout the day.

LEVEL ONE EMPATHY

There are levels to how we experience empathy. How many times have you gravitated toward particular people at a gathering because you thought, "They are my type of people"? Alternately, maybe friends set you up on a blind date with someone they claimed was your "perfect match" but halfway through the date you wondered what on earth your friends were ever thinking.

Level one empathy refers to the basic feeling of connection you feel with someone in response to external details. This type of empathy is what we feel when we think individuals will be compatible because of their appearance, social connections, line of work, and so forth. All of that is mostly surface information, but even so, this initial feeling of connection can be considered a basic level of empathy.

No doubt you started making this type of connection as a child: you saw someone in the schoolyard who looked like you in age, who dressed like you, and who talked somewhat like you, so you gravitated toward that student, thinking you might be friends. As we all know, this kind of connection sometimes works and other times leaves you dismayed. Yet many people, even those several decades into their professional lives, still rely this on this basic form of assessing people. You have probably been typecast by someone responding to you through this lens. Many times it does not generate big problems, but I would recommend digging deeper for more information and a stronger connection regarding any decision you flag as important.

LEVEL TWO EMPATHY

The next level of empathy involves thinking—rightly or wrongly—that you can feel what another individual is feeling. Let's say you see a woman crying. She explains that she has just broken up with her partner. You feel the kind of sadness that *you* would feel if you lost your romantic connection with your partner. But your empathy compass may be off; this can happen if your focus is too narrowly placed on yourself. For example, the woman may be crying because her partner took their golden retriever, not because she lost their romantic connection. What you, personally, are feeling is based on what you would have felt in a narrative based on your own experiences. Nonetheless, at this level of empathy, you attempt to feel as the other person might feel.

LEVEL THREE EMPATHY

At its next level, empathy delves into compassionate engagement: offering assistance. Your focus again goes to when you are or might be in a similar situation, but this time it proceeds to accurately grasp the other person's feeling(s). Even so, as you offer assistance, you are probably still considering what would soothe and balance *you* in a similar situation. In fact, your contribution may not be effective because what's comforting to another may not be the same as for you. For instance, some people have a rough workday and unwind by talking it over with a friend; others want quiet, privacy, and a long, warm bath.

There are also different types of the same emotion, which can misconnect you with someone at this level of empathy. Sometimes you won't see what another person needs because that precise type of emotion is not in your experience. You may, for example, understand fear but not the particular type of fear that a colleague is experiencing.

Let's say your colleague has been diagnosed with a serious illness. If your own life mantra is to always muscle through whatever is in your path, you may not be able to connect with his actual need for a gentler, less heroic path back to good health. He doesn't see himself as a warrior able to fend his problem off. He craves peace.

I can't tell you how many times I have heard advice given in an aggressive, albeit well-meaning, way. It often can do more harm than good. Moreover, when you don't recognize or you misinterpret someone's actual needs, the advice you do offer can sound like criticism. Instead of relieving their worries, you actually may be increasing their anxieties.[3] In such moments, well-intentioned compassion only adds to the problem. Level three empathy catches the general feeling experienced by others but sometimes may not connect with a constructive response.

LEVEL FOUR EMPATHY

At this level, all your empathy circuits come together effectively. They are able to meld with the other person's, and you are able to feel the world as that person does. You ask yourself what *that person* needs at the moment, and you can successfully grasp it. Level four empathy compassionately catches the general feeling experienced by others and is able to respond with what is best in the circumstance.

THE GOLDEN RULE

In his book *The Neuroscience of Fair Play: Why We (Usually) Follow the Golden Rule*, Dr. Donald Pfaff, known in the neuroworld for discovering the exact cellular targets for steroid hormones in the brain, theorizes that empathy can prevent us from harming ourselves as well as leading us to do good. It allows us to actually see ourselves in the position of the other person and the other in position of ourselves. This leads us to not want to do to the other person what we would not want done to ourselves.[4]

Your brain is wired with an automated motor memory part to empathy as well as a sensory capacity. Say I stop typing for a moment and instead I visualize myself typing the next sentence of this book. Even though my visualization might be blurry and at times may resemble a hologram, I know that I am the person who is performing the typing. I can see an image of myself doing it, and I can store that image in my memory and even see it in my mind again later. You can visualize yourself externally and internally, seeing yourself filling a customer order, per se, or conducting any task at work, and at the same time knowing what's going on inside your body and head as you do it. According to Pfaff's book, we are hardwired with such capacity, and this capability extends to when we observe another individual as well.[5] So not only can you sense what it's like to be in the position of another, but differently from, say, looking at a picture of another and recognizing what's going on, we are wired to literally feel it.

MONKEY SEE, MONKEY DO NEURONS

Mirror neurons, originally referred to as *monkey see, monkey do neurons*, were discovered by Italian scientist Giacomo Rizzolatti while researchers were in the process of monitoring a monkey's brain. As researchers were recording a particular circuit in the monkey's brain, one of the scientists realized that the neuron in question was firing whenever the monkey observed the researcher

holding his own arm in a certain position to grasp a cup of coffee. The monkey wasn't actually mimicking the movement, but its
brain was reacting as if it was doing so. The researchers concluded
that the monkey was responding to the scientist's actions. This
showed that neurons connected to the monkey's personal actions
could also connect to the actions of others. It was astonishing to
researchers because the monitoring showed that simply observing another's actions would fire neurons responsible for that
action in the brain of an observer.

Scientists came to realize that these mirroring circuits were
not just a monkey thing; they were also a human thing. Researchers additionally discovered that mirror neurons extended to
emotions as well, so when you sense that you are catching
another person's feelings, you often are. At first, research was
interested on how this mechanism could help people learn—
particularly motor skill activity. You see this type of learning in
babies. You raise your hand to a "high five" position and the baby
raises hers. You widen your eyes, and she widens hers. As we age,
we learn things like how to play a chord on a guitar; kick a soccer
ball; touch intimately; and express happiness, grief, displeasure,
or amazement. Linked to our empathy system, mirror neurons
deepen our ability to read thoughts, feel sensations, and imitate
physical actions belonging to others—and to treat others as we
wish to be treated ourselves.

Empathy helps us more strongly connect with other individuals and cogenerate positive experiences. Let's say you
approach a customer or coworker and are wearing the fact that
you are in a rush all over you: your words are short and quick,
your tone dismissive, and your movements rapid. First of all, the
other person can feel and understand all this in their body and
mind. Empathy, however, allows you, and the other person, to
experience the scene differently. You can opt to place your mind
in the other person's. You can attempt to perceive your actions

from that individual's perspective. You can feel what that person may feel as you encounter each other. You can ask yourself, "How do my thoughts and actions fit into the bigger picture of my relationship and into what I want to have happen next (my goal) at this juncture in the day?" Empathy circuits, supported by your mirroring capabilities, allow you to assess and edit your actions so that you can better deliver what's best for your relationship and goals.

TRY THIS!

Don't forget about yourself. Think about your mindfulness, self-awareness, attention, kindness, and goals. Think about your passions. Empathy applies to connecting with the person you are on the inside, too. Consider where you are, where you have been, and where you would like to be down the line.

Think in terms of making incremental changes, as we discussed in the previous chapter. Consider, for a moment, what it will feel like to be this future person. What other details will be in your life at that point? Consider the risk of NOT pursuing this dream. What will it feel like to be that person who did not take the risk? Who else may be affected along the way and further down the line? Let your empathy brighten your attention.

THE "OTHER" MOZART EFFECT

Your empathy machinery is also able to connect with nonhuman targets. It has long been known that it can, for example, attach to art or aesthetics. These feelings may consist of the empathetic understanding of what others feel as they are depicted within the art or more strikingly as an inward imitation of their observed actions in pictures and sculptures.[6] "The painting will move the soul of the beholder when the people painted there each clearly shows the movement of his own soul…we weep with the weeping, laugh with the laughing, and grieve with the grieving. These movements of the soul are known from the movements of the body."[7]

It's no wonder we love to experience art, from theater, poetry, and fiction to music, dance, painting, cinema, and electronic arts, as well as all the art forms yet to come. We love how art makes us feel. From the perspective of mind-body medicine, art can be used "medicinally" to make us feel exactly what we need at a certain moment in our lives, to get us out of or prevent us from falling into a funk, to make us remember exactly what we want to remember, and to make us feel and even understand things in advance that we have yet to feel or experience. And all of this exposure can better help us prepare to meet our daily living with a smarter, zeroed-in, and readied brain.

Recently my family attended an aesthetic-quenching performance by the Albany Symphony Orchestra. Their final pieces were from Mozart, whom we all love. For me, personally, it is Mozart's sudden, unexpected riffs that make his music so exciting. After the show, my wife made a comment about imagining what it might be like to enter Mozart's mind as it was once upon a time—as he may have played one of the pieces himself. What, oh what would you see and feel? I so enjoyed what she said, because to some extent, we *can* do that. Empathy circuits literally give us the capability to put ourselves into another's head and experience it with that person at various levels. What a way to copy-paste, if you will, different ways of seeing the world or solving problems. Turning your empathy circuits toward art can take you beyond just frequencies that stimulate and/or calm. It can spark new insight. It can teach you lessons. Sometimes you want to "catch" a specific behavior, whether it is from a character, within a painting, or from a song in order to make it part of your repertoire. Other times you do so because you can better understand a character's dysfunction and perhaps its consequences as well. Empathy can help you discover solutions previously unavailable to you.

 Let other people's feelings into your attention and don't forget about your own.

CHAPTER EXERCISES

Practicing the Golden Rule

As this chapter has shown, empathy is an important people skill that is related to your ability to listen to your emotions and others' and put these in sync with specific daily goals. By practicing the Golden Rule, you deepen your awareness and ability to predict the consequences of your own behavior and that of others'.

Before acting, take these steps.

1. Ask yourself, "What am I about to do?" See the action or behavior in your mind.
2. Next, ask yourself, "Who or what is the target of my action?"
3. Imagine a split-screen image of yourself and the other person(s) involved. Merge the two images (and minds) by bringing them closer together, adjusting your focus

by narrowing and widening it at times. The idea is to get the best understanding of what's going on in both minds.

4. Consider the action you are about to engage in from both perspectives—yours and the other person's.
5. Ask yourself, "Is this action right? Does it need modifying?" If it does not need modifying, then pursue it. Otherwise, put the brakes on and adjust it as needed.

You can engage this model on the fly or preset it in visualization. You can also edit it in a reflection after the experience. I recommend this step to update links and incorporate insights and any new learning. Consider your accomplishment and feel good about it. This will connect the model to your reward system.

Delaying Your Opinion

Next time a colleague is speaking, fight off the urge to have an immediate opinion. And even more so, resist the temptation to start talking about yourself and your personal experiences that may associate with the issue. Instead, get mindful, aware, and attentive to what the other person is saying. Place your focus on trying to understand the chain of that other person's reasoning as it applies to him or her. Consider the other person's goal. Consider what your goal is in the situation. Consider your joint goal. Then respond appropriately. The important thing is that your colleague feels listened to and to pay attention to what effect that may have on your working relationship with them. Afterward, you can build on that.

Using Art as Your Aesthetic

Consider a situation you are about to undertake that is of concern to you. Think of a song (lyrical or instrumental) you love that sends you a positive message you believe offers accurate guidance. Watch or listen to a video of the song as performed by a favorite musician on YouTube or download your song. Personally, I think this works best when the performer is also the writer. Using the split-screen technique in the Golden Rule exercise, merge your mind with the performer's. How would that individual want to be acting ideally in your targeted situation? Visualize this. Consider any thoughts that arise as possible ways of expanding your insights as you seek your best solution.

11

Can't Take My Eyes off of You

Rule #11

*Discover what's swaying your focus this
way or that. Eliminate negative influencers
and enhance the good ones.*

Whoever's not biased, sit! Why isn't everyone standing? The
reason biases can get the best of you is that hardly any of us, if
asked, would say we are biased.

Ever find yourself having to word a volatile email response
when you can't afford to be misinterpreted or flare up someone's
emotions on the other end? You finally think you *mostly* have
it, plus you've run out of time, and so send it. However, as the
day progresses you stress out about it, thinking of several better ways you could have responded. Your brain just won't let you
drop it. And now it's driving you—well, nuts. We all have biases.
A certain thought or action works out for you in one experience,
gets saved in your memory, and becomes your go-to solution
next time around in a similar situation. This process is usually

unconscious to you, so you operate pretty much fully updated without hassle. It increases your ability and efficiency when pursuing similar goals in the future. For this reason, our biasing network is hardwired and operates under your radar. It's supposed to help. But at times it can be a real pain.

You don't think much about how biases are weighing into workday decisions and performance. In fact, they can be triggered by infinite influencers, including environmental, organizational, and cultural triggers. Let's say you are a woman with a PhD in nuclear engineering. However, despite your solid background, your supervisor will not recommend you for promotion because your supervisor has been criticized in the past for advancing too many women in the department. She knows you would be the best individual for the job, but instead she is swayed to give the position to one of your less-qualified male colleagues. Your supervisor is in a quandary. The organization can't afford not having the best individual they can get in the position, yet at the same time they want to be fair. Perhaps the answer is in their policies. Perhaps they can generate other ways to achieve their goal of being fair.

Biases can also arise from a plethora of other sources, such as nationally reported business or political stories, culture, personal relationships, workplace dynamics, traditions, invading memories, and even objects like fancy pens versus standard pencils, as discussed in chapter 8. Unfortunately, your negative biases can cause you to react in disadvantageous ways; under the influence of such biases, you may see, access, and act upon information, thoughts, people, and situations in a harmful way that can then generate further problems. To manage influences that are restricting your daily performance, you must begin by identifying them. Then you can learn how to eliminate negative biases as well as how to utilize positive ones.

HOW DO YOU KNOW IF YOU ARE BIASED?

Let's start with this: we all are biased. Ever argue to do something a certain way just because this is the way you've always done it and that approach has worked in the past? Who hasn't? Perhaps you did the brunt of the work on a successful group project and now you find yourself taking on that role all of the time. Notice I didn't say you were leading the project—just doing most of the work! Or what about these examples? Ever have a mostly good day yet perceive the whole day as a bummer because of one relatively inconsequential element that didn't go your way? Do you ever get on a tangent of hurling negative remarks at just about anything? Or maybe you can't stop praising certain people almost as soon as you see them. Something just triggers in your head, and you do it. This is all the stuff of biases. And, without monitoring, these influencers will get in your way. Of course, like everything else in your attention system, they can contribute to your daily satisfaction, too.

Biases can be so strong that we may allow them to misrepresent the way we really feel and act. For example, psychologists have long known that people can go on record for liking or even voting for a certain political candidate and at the same time fib a little, telling their friends or coworkers that they actually like or voted for another candidate—usually the one who is more acceptable within their workplace or social cultures. Individuals may even change their story depending on the person they are talking to. Ever tell a joke one way to a certain group or individual and change it for another? Same thing. Most of us have gotten plenty of off-the-record advice from coworkers. But did you know that if you think what you are being told is in confidence, you'll be prone to take the advice? On the other hand, you usually act against advice that you know is trying to sway you. As soon as you start thinking that someone is trying to influence your opinion, you'll lean in the opposite direction. This is also a two-way street—something to consider, that is, when you are the one who is trying to sway others' actions.

Biases allow specific preconceptions to get imbedded in your mind unconsciously, which will affect your behavior and mind-sets down the line. It's natural to think that some ideas are worthier than others, more reasonable, more reliable, and sounder. Nothing wrong with that. But don't forget, brains are miserly. They strive to act quickly and efficiently—eliminating the need to think much.[1] As such, we pin solutions in our memory. Here's an example.

Someone I know often repeated a quote he'd heard from his grandfather: "The best sale is the one that gives you one hundred percent off because you don't buy anything at all." Whenever my acquaintance wanted to emphasize the importance of saving money as opposed to spending it, he'd pull the quote out. His mind was also preset toward pinching funds even when he could benefit from more liberal spending. Much too often, he missed out on deals for needed materials or services and wound up spending more organizational monies down the road to purchase them. Biases are like mental superglue, attaching your attention to certain details when they pop up and letting the rest go unnoticed. About the time he'd see the merits of loosening up, the opportunity had passed.

The element of bias is rooted in very old self-preservation drives that draw us to information, ideas, people, and memories that shore up our thoughts, feelings, and actions in a current moment. They support our general take on the world—but not always in a good way.

Biases like to kick in when things go wrong. We favor ourselves and our "tribe," and we generally find that fault is with the other side. If your beliefs feel threatened enough, this perception can fly you straight into attack mode. A colleague of mine, a psychiatrist, once told me no one she ever counseled regarding conflict resolution ever felt that they themselves were the cause of the problem. It was somehow always the other person's fault.

Biasing circuits evolved as another of nature's ways of hard-wiring us with a protective force field. At their best, they are responsible, at times, for your quick rejection of information and actions that may be harmful to you or others. On the other hand, they can cause you to reject paths vital to your goals and equally essential toward conveying the right, authentic image of you as a person. Mindful awareness and attention can help.

TRY THIS!

Visualization is a very effective way of dealing with editing or eliminating biases. Next time you have an important situation coming up, use visualization to generate some presets the night before. Picture yourself operating in the upcoming circumstance. Pause within the picture to examine why you are making certain choices; this will expose biases at play. It will help you check your reasoning as you choose one action over another. Ask yourself, "Is there some element (possibly an emotion) tugging at me that seems unrelated? Is it automatically triggered? Is that information or feeling my own, or is it based on someone else's perspective? If it belongs to someone else, what about the source? Is my source's perspective on the situation accurate, reasonable, and applicable to me? How so? Do I want it bearing influence on me? If not, why? If it is my own, is it reasonable within the circumstances I am examining? What alternate thoughts or actions might be relevant? Use this information to begin laying out your strategy.

THE CHIP IN YOUR MEMORY

Biases in a sense work like *computer chips* imbedded below your radar, controlling what information you pull out of your memory files and exactly what spin you'll put on them. But they can also mess with your memories as you attempt to recall them. Ever remember, for instance, the same event differently over time? For me, a prime example would be the attacks of 9-11. I can remember exactly where I was that day as I saw the reports on the news. First thing I did was rush to tell my wife, who was in another room. My memory of what I'd seen was decent at that point. But I cannot be sure of how accurate the incident is in my head today. As with so many other incidents in life, my memory of it has become contaminated, so to speak, with other media versions (now part of my memories) of the same event. As far as 9-11 is concerned for me and most Americans, we have seen its footage countless times over the years. We have viewed it from different angles, we have discussed it in different contexts, and we have made many different points of it. My current memory of the tragedy still seems sharp as ever, but realistically, it is probably closer to a composite than to what I actually witnessed and felt the morning of Tuesday, September 11, 2001.

Another reason you may recall experiences differently depends on the point you want to make. Your theme, so to speak, becomes a bias. It operates like a zombie to assemble the rest of your memory, editing the narrative wherever necessary to crystallize your point. You fill in gaps in the story line or images with self-created script. For instance, if you are trying to prove that a specific coworker is highly motivated, you might recall a specific task that person went all out on and use that memory to illustrate your point. If, on the other hand, you are trying to prove that this specific coworker has a domineering, aggressive personality, you might just as well remember the same event but fill in the narrative as you go along with details (factual or not) to show the person dominating the situation. In effect, we shape our memories to serve the point de jour.

What's more, tangential details of certain events, especially emotional ones, can trigger you years later. For instance, seemingly out of nowhere, a bias can be triggered in a millisecond by scents like particular perfumes, the color of autumn leaves, the image of sun pouring through the windows in your office at a certain angle during a particular season, or a song suddenly playing in a store. All of these biases can influence your next thought or feeling.

Environmental details are so powerful, in fact, they can drive your attentional machinery for the rest of your life. As such, your memory recall is subject to constant biases. You can be manipulated by these like a drone, or you can regulate them advantageously. Later in this chapter you'll see how you can use biases to give you great energy, focus, and increased memory for daily goals.

Memory, thanks to nature, associates with your ability to learn from your biases and to use what you've learned in making positive adjustments toward future goals. When you acknowledge that an action—your own or another person's, even actions of a fictional character—works to accomplish a positive result, your understanding is stored in a memory file, and with it a host of updated links to help guide you in similar future situations. Consequently, the hope in self-regulation and attention training is that learning from your biases triggers problem-solving thoughts and actions toward similar goals down the line. Your job is to become aware of the role of biases within the things you do and to learn from them, then edit, eliminate, or create effective updated links for future use. In order to do this, you need to remain open to the possibility.

TRY THIS!

The magic phrase for this exercise is "Sure…but wait!" Here's how it works. When you first are confronted with information that rattles your point of view, and your immediate reaction is to attack it, think, "Sure…" You may be right (regarding your own point of view). The opposing perspective may well be inaccurate or all wrong. But then add "…but wait!" In fact, the other person may be absolutely right—in a way you haven't yet considered. Use the mantra as a lighthearted reminder to pause and consider the opposing view. Question the individual(s) for clarity on the opposition if necessary. The idea is to open up to the other perspective, the one you would have almost certainly denied to your attention. Then use all available information to select the best alternative for your goal. Afterward, reflect on what can be learned from the process itself. Acknowledge positive outcomes as rewards. This will further weaken the initial reactive bias and make your new approach stronger and quicker next time.

THE BIAS OF RISK

It's generally human nature to make choices based on what we think presents the least risk so we can try to pursue the simpler approach to achieve our goal. Here, memory plays into the equation once again. As we've discussed, we naturally update experiential links after situations to reemphasize or even change certain details. When we do, we tend to reduce and preserve daily events in memory as key points. These can include information points that are cold (nonemotional), warm (emotional), or hot (emotional) as well as unexpected details and teachable elements. Let's look at an example.

Anthony's coworkers often fling around sarcastic "hot" references to be funny. Anthony has done so himself on more than one occasion, and he has enjoyed the laughs. He will be rethinking that behavior from now on, however, because his sarcasm on a sensitive subject recently upset Lori, a coworker. Although Anthony had gotten caught up in and engaged in the office bias, the incident became a teachable moment for him—because he made it so. To accomplish this, he had to first fight off his own biased urges to think, "Hey—well, everyone else is sarcastic! Why shouldn't I be? Besides, Lori should know when I'm kidding." He had to get past thinking it was the other person's fault. He had to visualize how such biases had triggered words to come out of his mouth that don't necessarily represent who he is. And he had to be motivated to change that. With practice, Anthony was able to eliminate the risk factor of these biases by presetting a bias *against* being sarcastic in the office.

Because you rely on memory files, you automatically filter memories aggressively to reduce the quantity of information you have to deal with. As we've discussed, you fill in gaps, you change information to suit a current point, and you remember bits and pieces to make your theme. As a result, you miss things. Sometimes you may find that, like Anthony at the start of this story, you can shoot yourself in the foot by having a memory link that reinforces and engages specific errors of judgment. But also like Anthony, you have the ability to recalculate these links and replace them with better ones. Your job is to identify negative biases and alter them to work toward your goals rather than against them.

HALOS AND BANDWAGONS

Most of us become overconfident in our estimation of outcomes. Overconfidence is a form of bias, and it affects our thinking and behavior. One way we do this is to bind things together with positive qualities where they may or may not exist. Psychologists call this the *halo effect*.[2] You may see, for example, one attractive quality in an individual, and then that triggers you to look for others. For example, if you decide that a stranger looks fit and handsome, you may conclude that he must also be smart and athletic. Similarly, if a town looks quaint and picturesque, you may conclude that the residents are hospitable or that it would be a nice place to live.

At times we find ourselves jumping on board when and where most people in our peer group or our culture—workplace and otherwise—seem to be opining on a certain issue. For instance, if most people are voting for a greater pay raise yet fewer health insurance benefits, then it's easier to "catch" the same opinion despite evidence that the contrary may be the better choice. This is a form of bias psychologists refer to as the *bandwagon effect*.

Similar to group bias, in which we tend to favor members of our own tribe (or group), we tend to view outsiders as inferior. Problematically, you can become blind to the good in other choices and simultaneously strengthen your lure to finding and sticking to information that sustains your particular thinking and beliefs—even if that information is faulty. This form of bias makes you vulnerable to the old "tell them what they want to hear" trickery. If your group is made up of Second Amendment advocates, for instance, you become vulnerable to statistics that indicate that gun regulation doesn't do much to lower crime; the reverse is true if your group is for more controlled licensing.

We are mostly biased to maintain the status quo—our own, our group's, and our extended group's. Most individuals don't want to rock the boat and specifically our own position on it. But the irony is that we, like Anthony, may be letting our goals be rocked without realizing it when our biases engage without our monitoring.

As humans we want to sustain our integrity, and we are motivated to do so. So another way we learn to keep flowing is by maintaining a status quo of what we perceive as our self-worth. Examples might include, "I run a successful law practice"; "The companies I represent can count on me to protect and advocate for them"; "I am creative"; or "I am a community leader."

If we feel our self-profile has been threatened, we tend to denigrate the message or messenger. We may become defensive and sometimes outright aggressive. Simultaneously, we look for detail to confirm our self-portrait, so to speak. Known as *confirmation bias,* this tendency makes certain individuals become overly defensive when they are made aware of a potential risk in the way their actions are being conceived and conducted.

Confirmation bias is especially of concern if your work sometimes places you in higher-risk decision making situations. "It is not surprising that people exhibit defensiveness, given that they appear to be motivated to hold positive self-views."[3] The problem is that once you get defensive, you are more likely to dismiss valuable information. Your attention is off somewhere else, looking to restore your integrity.

Consider the time when your boss delivered critical feedback sandwiched between two compliments. It's not always easy, but you can flow around the negative vibes that might be creeping up on you, keeping your sense of balance. Self-integrity can be restored by affirming an equally important source of self-worth not connected to the threat or warning. In that way, cues that affirm your profile can be set accordingly. If you have been affirmed, then you tend to be less defensive about the message. You'll listen more and be more open. You'll devote more attentional control to threatening material. You'll show more engagement with material you might otherwise dismiss.[4] This approach helps to avoid mishap as well as error.

Self-affirmation, mood, self-esteem, and other directed feelings are interrelated. What's more, all this becomes cognitive, going into learning and memory to be applied and further strengthened in time as it continues to be applied and updated. It doesn't remove defensive behavior; rather the bias affects it at important stages, such as not turning off to something important that can make a difference. It can allow you to perceive a specific behavior differently. This helps you produce positive attitudinal changes.

The more you affirm other aspects of character—such as your skill as an artist, writer, musician, athlete, and so on—the more resilient you become and the more you empower the "self" in self-integrity. You might even create a resume to highlight the power of your vocational skill set; this task can help open you up to putting better attention on your risky career-related behaviors. The hope is to avoid and replace them with more poignant, goal-facilitated actions.

TRY THIS!

Practice the technique of self-affirmation by identifying your most important value and how it is expressed in you, things you do, and things you could be doing. Self-affirmation can be situationally specific. Let's say you identify that what's important to you about your profile is that as a PR leader you can successfully brand an organization. You can combine the practice of self-affirmation with reflection, reflecting on your most satisfied clients and ways you helped them crush this goal, and focus on similar ways you can help clients in the future.

OPTIMISM BIAS

Optimism bias is a type of bias that, in general, has us thinking we are less likely to experience a negative event or outcome to what we do. The phrase "When life hands you lemons, make lemonade" captures the more general meaning of optimism bias as a sort of positive thinking. More specifically, however, optimism bias is understood as being exclusively directed toward the future, not present or past experiences or actions. Your motivation to hit a rewarding goal down the line is linked to these expectancies.[5] Also associated with your optimism for how endeavors turn out is *wanting* the reward for nailing them, *liking* the pleasure of achieving the reward, and subsequently *learning* how to achieve the reward so you can do it again. Great benefits can be obtained by a normal influence of this bias. It helps keep you flowing toward hitting each rung on the ladder to get you to your goals. It's a great loop of motivation.

With that in mind, you have to watch out. An extremely optimistic mind-state can get you into trouble. It can make risky choices look attractive, because you are so convinced that everything will work out in the end. You might take on an unhealthy level of work-related travel, for instance. Similarly, your biased optimism may be messing with your ability to hit a healthy budget, work on teams, or endorse an organizational policy. Outside of work, people who get trapped in this mind-set can find themselves taking too many vitamins or pushing themselves to work out to the extreme because they overoptimistically believe that more of a good thing will be beneficial.[6]

Consider the following situation. Maxine worked for a large employer. One year, her organization put the word out that they needed several individuals from her department who would be willing to undergo a certification training program. She learned that if she became certified, she could take on a new position in the company as an HR miniclass instructor. Her new position would involve visiting organizational sites around the country, providing a variety of necessary training classes for employees. Her immediate impression was that it sounded like a lot to take on. During her whole life, however, she'd operated under the notion that she should "never look a gift horse in the mouth," especially when it had the potential to make life sweeter. Consequently, she accepted the offer. "It may be fun," she rationalized, looking to the positive.

Upon completion of the training, Maxine was rewarded with a spike in salary and generous words about more job security from her supervisor. Although she wasn't sure if she wanted to remain with this employer for the long run, she rationalized again with thoughts that she did like the idea of more permanence. Her motivations, expectations, future estimations, and the fact that she liked and wanted more security did take her eye off looking for another possible professional career, one that might have better matched her passions and was closer to her dreams. However, she liked not having to think about or pursue job searching—even though it could possibly introduce her to a more satisfying career and could provide sweeter "food for the soul." Her bias for job security for the long haul was leading her to stay with the HR miniclass position.

For the next several years, she found it comforting to just follow the prefabricated plan. Rewards included more salary increases and more kind words of job security, as well as positive expectations of climbing up the proverbial corporate ladder. However, one day without much warning, the organization liquidated her job. They closed down all corporate operations in her part of the country. She was left thinking, "Why did I do all that?" Her own bias had played a strong role in driving her right to where she, years before, would have never thought she would wind up. You could say her biases betrayed her.

Do decisions and expectations always have to turn out this way? No. But you need to take care so they don't. Remember, biased thinking is wired into us. Regular self-awareness scans will help you avoid waking up one day far from where you were headed when you were following your passions. When was the last time you felt like you were following your dream? This is a vital question we each need to ask as we paint the canvas of our career and living. Stay aware. Check in with your inner self often.

Because optimism bias will guide your attention to specific details that you expect will deliver reward, it is a powerful influencer. As such, it can trump even a strong top-down cue. Let's return to Anthony's example. You may recall that he offended Lori with his jokes. In part, he initially associated the momentary reward of telling an off-color joke with a way to achieve workplace stress reduction because he overoptimistically believed his humor would be well appreciated by *all* of his coworkers. In this way, his optimism superseded a self-cue he had personally ingrained in his head to avoid offensive speech at work, so he needed to step back, learn from his mistake, and deliberately change his behavior for the future. Your job is to eliminate some of the misguidance of this biasing network.[7]

On the positive side, a healthy dose of optimism bias can reduce stress and provide higher levels of self-esteem, confidence, and flow. It will keep your mind and energy in the game. Optimism bias helps you detect potentially advantageous, goal-related information in an environment where there is a lot of detail competing for your attention. What's more, the bias, its rewards, and its triggers will strengthen when you link them to your memory of where your attention effectively aimed in successful experiences. This will help you in the future whenever you pursue a similar goal because this link will serve as a preset pattern to successfully guide your behavior. You will establish biasing circuits that work to your advantage.

WHEN OPTIMISM BETRAYS

Once your emotional system starts weighing into your task-achievement and optimistic bias machinery, it can further drive your motivations toward expecting certain rewards—as Maxine came to enjoy her boss's praise and support, the increases in salary, and the general sense of comfort it all gave her. This combination can drive your attention away from almost any potential risks to your behaviors. Let's say you desire what you're going after, you like it, you're motivated to pursue it, you'll denigrate any idea that conflicts or warns against it, you'll attack disagreeing ideas if you have to, and you will overestimate outcomes. Sounds like you're all in, right? You are. But while you don't want to succumb to depression and pessimism—the opposite of this bias—you still need to take care that you don't call off your sensitivity to risk entirely. Ultimately, you want to strike a balance of optimism, positivity, and a realistic awareness of risk so you can effectively pay attention to and pursue the very advantageous details that will sweeten your work and career. It's always worth stepping back and asking yourself, "Is there strong evidence for the successful implementation of an alternate approach to a current task or goal? If so, what are the steps for me to implement it?" Be optimistic, but have an insurance plan.

From the perspective of mind-body medicine, keeping a mind-state of positive expectation regardless of outcome makes you happier throughout a process and at the end of it. Anticipation enhances your well-being. Without it, we'd all be depressed. The thrill of the wait is important, and it makes the payoff prettier. Perhaps this is why most people find that scheduling a fun activity for a Friday is preferable to planning it for a Sunday because it gives you something to look forward to afterward, whereas Sunday only gives you work on Monday to look forward to.[8] Don't shortchange yourself. Enjoy the process.

You need to be able to see yourself getting the job done and be optimistic about the outcome—see it turning out well. If your brain does not expect good results, it does not have an alarm telling it, "Wrong solution." It will fail to learn from its mistakes, and it will be less likely to improve life for you. Remember, negative expectations shape outcomes in a negative way. For instance, if you think that pursuing an alternate career will be too complex to navigate, you'll conclude that you shouldn't go for it. Think back to the statistics cited at the beginning of this book regarding job satisfaction and recognition of talents:

- 55 percent of workers in the United States report feeling stressed on their job.
- More than half of US workers are dissatisfied with their jobs.
- 82 percent of us feel our strongest talents go wasted.

And their related problems of:

- Worker absenteeism, tardiness, and burnout
- Decreased productivity
- Workers' compensation claims
- Increased employment turnover
- Medical insurance costs from work-related stress

The last thing I want is for you to fall into that conundrum. And you don't have to. Instead, you can take the next step toward your dreams.

Make discovering what's biasing your focus a priority, especially in important daily situations. Eliminate negative influencers and utilize positive ones.

CHAPTER EXERCISES

Using Visualization

Use visualization to generate a positive bias by seeing yourself acting positively, in a self-regulated way, in a circumstance you wish to control. Repeat the visualization often prior to the real-time situation.

Using Optimism Bias to Influence Others Toward a Certain Mind-set or Action

Optimism can guide others more strongly than punishment.[9] Your happy face can direct someone toward positive motivation and detail more than your expression of concern or worry. Remind yourself today to let your contentment show.

Exposing an Unconscious Bias

Using reflection, examine how quickly you lost your temper in a specific situation or judgment call or how quickly you came to a positive feeling or action that led you to take a disadvantageous action. Ask yourself, "What triggered my response?" Consider your options for alternate responses. Visualize each alternative within the scenario. Choose the best option and repeat the visualization several times. Use the visualization to help preset your reactions before a similar upcoming event.

12

Keep a Little Soul

Rule #12

*Cool off your busy circuits before they shut you
down. Refresh your energy throughout the day and
especially during the evening so you can wake up
restored and ready to greet the next day.*

Mental fatigue is a common problem in the workforce. Similarly, the potential for a good night's sleep will go up in smoke
quickly if there are overworked mental circuits eating up your
headspace. Just like muscles, whether driven by positive or negative motivators, these circuits need to cool down. This is especially true when your focus has been warding off stressors and
has been concentrated for long periods. As this chapter will discuss, developing a good restorative routine to use while at work
and afterward is important.

From a holistic perspective, your attentional needs will bear
your unique fingerprints. Let's look at two examples of people
who need to refresh themselves in different ways.

Justine likes her career and deals with the work environment fairly well. Intellectually, she gets along with her colleagues, and she doesn't get stressed out much or experience burnout very often. When she goes home for the evening, she wants to slow down, reward herself with a nice meal with her family, chill, get some good sleep, and wake up refreshed for the next day.

In contrast, Lee doesn't really enjoy his employment. He is constantly driven by negative feelings throughout the day, and his brain is taxed by bursts of neurochemicals that heighten Lee's compulsions to rehash off-putting experiences that keep popping up in his life. He typically sees these situations as coming at him, never the other way around. Consequently, his brain spends a lot of its workday full of chemical and emotional thoughts. These relentlessly focus on individuals and circumstances that, as Lee sees it, continue to mess and stress him. When he arrives home for the evening, like Justine, he wants to unwind pleasantly with his family. Instead, like clockwork the atmosphere nosedives into his gripes about colleagues he thinks are awful and wrecking his life. Dinners are often short and not communal. He drinks a little over his limit to de-stress, enough to reduce his quality of sleep. He is in dire need of strategies that will help reverse this cycle. Additionally, his circuits for empathy and social awareness are often running on low. His attention's executive function is not controlling his activity patterns, and instead, over time, his emotions have been taking over.

Both brains are fatigued. Each person, however, needs a different method of balancing to refresh these brain circuits. It makes sense for Justine to attempt to develop an activity pattern that will help her brain wind down. It also is sensible for her to engage in activities that will sustain her already positive perspective and performance at work. She is a good candidate for the motto "Keep on keeping on." She simply needs to revitalize so she can maintain the good daily road she is already on. In contrast, Lee may want to engage in activities that will help him change his mental activity. He could benefit from generating new patterns of thinking and acting to replace the constant negative emotions that are controlling his day and preventing him from having restorative evenings.

THE BRAIN'S RESTING ZONE

Allowing your brain a chance to rest throughout the day and evening is a priority. Revitalization opportunities allow brain circuits that have been peeling out and leaving rubber all day not only to cool down but also to more easily slip into the refreshing flow-state that resting brains like to explore. To wrap your mind around this concept, consider daydreams. You sit back, rest your mind, and relax your thoughts in a way that your mind can flow deeply into the past and future as if you were watching a movie. You see yourself accomplishing your dreams, such as becoming a successful leader, joining the ranks of your most admired colleagues, flowing through your work, and performing your tasks optimally and happily.

This resting-yet-flowing mind-set boosts your empathy circuits, allowing you to see certain daily tasks and goals from other people's perspectives as well as from your own. (You can even observe your goals from the viewpoint of fictional characters you may admire.) At rest, your mind can discover interrelationships among situations, details, and people, including details that are not necessarily apparent to you when you are operating in the fast pace of real time. In its resting zone, your mind can often more clearly connect personal needs, goals, and options. This mind-set can also revitalize your external focus circuits when you return to them. Consequently, your ability to mindfully capture this state and slip into it intentionally is worth its weight in gold.

TRY THIS!

I recommend using this refreshing technique whenever you have been concentrating too long or whenever you start to feel stuck on a single thought or feeling. Try to catch yourself just before the mind-set becomes locked.

Start by resting your mind and opening your attention to a wider lens. Relax your breathing and daydream a comfortable image, such as a warm, summery, still-water lake with sparkling sunlight glistening across it. See the myriad of reflections across its surface but don't attach your focus to any of them. Do the same with any thoughts, images, or feelings that come to mind. Acknowledge them, but keep your lens wide open and let them just float by on their way out of sight. Repeat as long as you are comfortable.

MATCH YOUR ENERGY

There is an arc, a rhythm per se, to the way mental and physical energy move through your mind and body and through your day. Your attentional strength as a result may, at times, spike with high energy bursts and, at other times, provide you with a deep sense of calm. Matching the right energy with a task is similar to switching from giving a PowerPoint presentation to rearranging the room's heavy furniture for another meeting. Each task has its own energy requirements. The idea is to self-regulate your energy so that it matches your goals.

When you don't self-regulate your energy, you cause yourself mental and physical stress. You consume more energy than you are cultivating. Your focus dulls, fatigues, and perhaps burns out. When you get the right match, however, you keep your energy flowing. In fact, your segue from one task to another will have its own energy requisite to keep your mind flowing seamlessly, so here too conscious regulation and increased sensitivity are key.

We are all prone, at times, to feeling somewhat like Justine—steady on an even keel. There are also moments, however, when we may be vulnerable to feeling like Lee.—trapped in our own patterns of negativity. And, of course, there are endless variations between. To effectively self-regulate your energy and match it appropriately to tasks, you should step back periodically. Make yourself aware of the status of your attention circuits and the energy requirements of your next task. Once you've identified these, you can pick out techniques we've discussed throughout the book to help get you there. Then, I recommend putting them into practice. The more you pair these, the sooner the techniques will link and ingrain. Soon they will automatically and efficiently evolve to fuel your attentional needs and keep your circuits happy throughout your day.

At the core of all mind-body improvement—at the heart of all improvement of the human spirit—is attention. Without it, we run the risk of operating as drones.

In lieu of chapter exercises, below is a daytime and a nighttime plan to help keep you feeling fresh and cool-minded. I encourage you to combine, experiment with, and practice these techniques to achieve the most benefits toward your own unique daily needs. Each morning, you will hit the ground running. Remember, things will not always match your expectations, but if you remain flexible and keep good links flowing, positive results will come.

DAYTIME PLAN

Pause and get out of your head every so often. Regularly use your pause button to step back and mindfully assess things before you transition into your next daily activity. You can do this just for a few brief moments indoors, or you might like to enhance the process by going outdoors for a short walk or snack. Consider adding an athletic activity, like jogging. You don't have to be located in a pristine environmental setting, although if you are I encourage you to use it. Otherwise, environmental imagery in the form of office artwork, photographs, internet videos, and photography works just fine. Your brain will respond either way, restoring your focus and drive. If you can design your own workspace, don't forget about ways you can enhance this element. The payoff will be rewarding. Regardless, whether you are outdoors tapping real natural environments or indoors using environmental imagery, either will help de-stress, balance emotions, and revitalize focus. Just pausing to look out your window can do the trick. I recommend using this practice often throughout the day.

Daydream. Make dreaming part of your daily routine. Take a break just to look at what you dream for your future. Relax your focus—take the tension out—and look at past and current moments you have relished. Exploring where you could go as a next step in your future can be fun, enlightening, and invigorating. Ask yourself, "What would the next steps look like?" Examine them freely from a variety of angles, from your own perspective, and from other people's perspectives. Consider a couple of creative paths you might really enjoy to reaching these goals. This way, both the road and the accomplishment can each be their own reward. Thinking out of the box—out of comfort zones—can be exciting.

Get yourself into a flow-state. Start with resetting yourself to your relaxed mind-set. Whether you're headed toward fatigue, beginning to make errors, or feeling emotionally down, you need to stop the funk dead in its tracks. Personally, my first-choice influencer is to tap the raw power of music that conveys the lyrical and rhythmic message I need to reset those moments. Pick a favorite song that emphasizes the message you need to hear and gets you back to the right groove. Ask yourself questions such as these: "Do I need something relaxing because I'm headed for burnout? Or do I need a dose of gangster rap to crank myself up?" Maybe you need an open, upbeat instrumental piece with no message to roam around and loosen up in. Consider using all three. Hit the repeat button until you arrive in a flow-state.

Massage your acupressure points. This form of gentle massage can quickly dissolve your mental fog and get you back in the flow. My absolute favorite is the *bubbling well,* which we discussed in chapter 7. Take a few daily moments and feel the magic there.

There are also acupressure points that run in a line down your forearms. Massage these points with your fingertips, starting about two inches above the elbow and tapping down the top of each forearm and back up. With a little practice, you will feel a precise line of points as you do this. You can use the same procedure up and down the outside length of each leg. Another point that releases calm and revitalizing energy is located at the center of your chest. You should find that lightly massaging this area with the fingertips of your right hand feels refreshing. You might try these massages as a mental and emotional cleanse before, during, or after you listen to music. Just don't overdo it.

Practice this two-minute Eastern movement. I call this activity *finger painting,* and it's great to do this indoors or out. Start by relaxing your breathing, then follow these steps.

- From a standing position, very slowly palm-paint a circle *clockwise*. At its completion, slowly step forward with your left foot. Stay in that position—left foot forward.
- From that position—left foot still forward—slowly palm-paint a circle *counterclockwise*. At its completion, slowly step forward with your right foot.
- Be mindful. Shut everything else out of your mind and concentrate on your movement as though it is the only thing that matters in your world at the moment.
- From that position—right foot still forward—repeat the whole pattern, painting *clockwise*.
- Keep the pattern going, reversing sides each time.

Use art. This step is similar to placing music on your electronic device so you can access it to adjust your mood whenever you need it. In this case, you select and store paintings, poetry, fiction, and nonfiction that convey the messages you need to hear. Using your electronic device for storage ensures that you will have easy access to more positive energies to maintain a flowing mind-set. This practice is perfect for sending transformative messages and energy to your brain at strategic points in your day. After reviewing your material, you can bring your charged mind and body back to work tasks. Your mind-set will transfer into what comes next.

Use stronger brews when needed. Combine techniques from this book—such as visual cues (images), auditory cues (music), and language cues (words or narratives)—to send yourself stronger, more affecting, and targeted messages. The more parts of your brain you target, the stronger the effect. Additionally, the more situationally specific the "brew" is to your goal, the better.

NIGHTTIME PLAN

Relax and refresh with music. On your way home, decide what kind of energy you need to balance off. Are you running on high energy and need to bring yourself down a bit so you'll feel relaxed when you arrive home? Or do you need to bring yourself up to a higher energy? Maybe you need to shift moods.

Relax and refresh into the environment. You can relax and recharge your circuits with a walk or other outdoor activity. I highly recommend participating in outside activities after work whenever conditions permit. Here too you can use music to segue from worktime to outdoor activity time and even throughout the activity. Consider having a prepared playlist that you can use every day. This will condition your mind and body to start segueing on their own both mentally and biologically.

I also recommend having your special, recharging activity picked out in advance. In fact, it makes sense to have an alternate activity as well because you may need to rely on it for multiple reasons (e.g., you are only available at a different time of day, one location is better in certain weather or traffic conditions, one activity has a stronger impact on you, and so forth).

The idea is to get out of your head and let a tried-and-tested environment you love get you flowing in a stream of clean, positive, non-work-focused energy. Then transfer this energy into your evening.

You can use a music playlist afterward to further define this feel-good energy by playing a lyric that sends your mind the exact message of where you want it to be. I call mine "Happy to Be Home." It includes the following material: "Doin' It Right" by

Daft Punk; "My Girl" by the Temptations; "Dance to the Music," an extended mix by Sly; "All You Need Is Love" by the Beatles; and "Keep a Little Soul" by Tom Petty and the Heartbreakers.

Relax and recharge into a slow dinner. Eat healthier and tastier foods. Put your attention on their pleasure and benefits. Have a relaxing dinner. Take care to slow down and, if you are with friends, your partner, or your family, make yourself mindful of their positive presence in your life. Put your attention on things about them that you enjoy.

Relax and refresh into some real talk. Have some genuine conversations during dinner or call a friend. Talk about solutions to any problems that may be popping up. Sometimes—often—that's the first step to seeing a solution. But don't get bogged down in the problem; rather, enjoy the support of others in solving it. Spend some time sharing dreams with others. Their positive vibes will transfer into your next day.

Meditate. Feel your energetic connection to yourself and to all of life. The following is a meditation I have used for decades and have taught many individuals. Perhaps you will enjoy trying it. Start by slowing down and deepening your breathing. Repeat the words aloud or in your mind "I am here" as you breathe in and "Here is now" as you exhale. Next, place your hand on your heart and feel its rhythm. Then, extend your attention outward beyond your body. Move it through all material things in your environment (e.g., walls, trees, clouds) and then outward toward the stars, through the stars and beyond, past the last lights, and finally into and past the last dark. Hold that mind-set for a while. Then slowly retrace your tracks back to where you began.

Read an inspirational book. Lastly, just before bedtime, consider reading something philosophical or spiritual to uplift your spirit with positivity. Choose something that makes you feel positive about yourself and about tomorrow...your future.

 Learning about how you want to feel and perform at work has a lot to do with examining how you are feeling and what's running under your radar that is responsible for the way your experiences unravel. When you trace the footprints of your distractions, you can discover among the sparks and circuits who you really are. When you change the way you are paying attention, you will get more comfortable with your true self. You can formulate decisions that make the moments, days, and weeks more satisfying and exciting. You can preset your mind and body to bring the best of you to the next level. The wonderment of this process is that it guides you toward conscious transformation. Good attention can be a choice. Use yours to evolve willfully, creatively, and prosperously.

FOR YOUR CONTINUED PRACTICE

You can practice the 12 rules of attention one at a time until they ingrain and begin to flow naturally. You can also consult them whenever slipups and other work-related issues arise. Find the specific rules that most pertain to your situation. Reread related chapters, and consider the tools within to help you refresh and rebalance.

Rule #1

Talk to your brain. Tell it you want it to pay attention to *how* you are paying attention.

Rule #2

Awareness, mindfulness, and attention are not the same thing. Use each individually to strengthen the others and significantly lighten up and improve the way you perform and feel.

Rule #3

Renovate your mind's automatizations to stay on top of your game. Your brain loves automatic triggers. You can't live without them. They make decisions easy, fast, and seemingly harmonious. Use them to your advantage.

Rule #4

Use your brain's capacity to identify and squash details that are disconnected to your goals.

Rule #5

Learn from the big and small (yet amazing) brains in nature.

Rule #6

Widen your attentional spotlight regularly to help catch important peripheral data.

Rule #7

Strengthen your attention span.

Rule #8

Manage what you don't see if it has an effect on your goals.

Rule #9

Know when to concentrate your attention vs. when to open it wide.

Rule #10

Remember the Golden Rule.

Rule #11

Discover what's swaying your focus this way or that. Eliminate negative influencers and enhance the good ones.

Rule #12

Cool off your busy circuits before they shut you down. Refresh throughout the day and especially during the evening so you can wake up restored and ready to greet the next day.

GLOSSARY

activation—to engage, trigger

adrenaline—a stress hormone secreted by the adrenal glands or in sync with exerted effort

algorithms—if/then problem solving instruction or guideline; if this circumstance appears then do that

alpha waves—brain waves that engender a feeling of calm alertness that is reflective and attentive—selectively concentrating on information

amplitude—how loud a sound is, the strength of the sound or wave

Arcy-sur-Cure—series of caves in north central France

attention—an electrochemical fetching mechanism targeting a piece of information, bringing it into your working memory and connecting it to other information you have stored there to create processes to accomplish your needs

attentional spotlight—describes field of attention and how it operates

auditory stream segregation—the separation of streams of sound in order to perceive what they are attached to in a scene

automatic pilot—when you are performing actions without thinking about it

automatizations—behaviors that have become automatic, automatic circuits that trigger these behaviors awareness—a consciousness that extends beyond the periphery of your attentional spotlight

bandwagon effect—a form of bias in which one aligns (jumps on board) with the majority or behaves a certain way because that's what most people are doing

beginner's mind—a concept of Zen Buddhism (also used in holistic medicine and arts) that says if you want to learn something well, you must first attain the simple focus of a novice whose mind is empty of bias and negativity and is fresh

beta—brain wave, the brain activity of the waking state

big picture—full representation of a situation, including internal and external perspectives

bottom-up processing—information processing guided by data input

BPM—beats per minute in a song

brain waves—electrical currents in the brain

bubbling well—acupuncture point at the center of the sole of the foot, about two-thirds of the way up from the heel to the base of the toes

choice blindness— phenomenon that causes people to be unable to accurately recall choices made

clear/repeat—empty mind, then proceed to attend to next task

close the gate—adjusting your mind to filter out irrelevant or overloading data from entering your attention

cognitive energy—mental energy

cognitive miser—the brain's tendency to use the least mental effort

conjugation—transfer of genetic material

halo effect— form of bias, overconfidence in our estimation of outcomes affecting thinking and behavior cortisol—a stress hormone

cue—internal or external guide to prompt behavior

currency—mental and physical energy

delta—brain wave(s), the brain activity that occurs with deep, dreamless sleep; the frequency associated with trances

descriptive detail—sensory detail

dissonance—a core element of music; refers to beats, sounds, harmonies, and rhythms that seem "off" or irregular or incomplete

DNA base pairs—the bases that form what look like "steps" of a "ladder" in the double helical structure of DNA

dopamine—the body's feel-good hormone (associated with feelings of euphoria)

EEG—Electroencephalogram, recording of electrical activity in and across the brain

EEG sensors—electrodes on different areas of the scalp

emotional intelligence—understanding your own feelings as well as your empathy for the feelings of others, the ability to self-regulate your emotions so they enhance your living

empathy—the ability to feel what other people are feeling, which allows you to predict the consequences of your actions

empty mind—a concept and technique that allows you to bypass stress, attachments, and negative feelings

energy—informed-power

estrogen—steroid sex hormone commonly associated with women

executive attention—attention's CEO, has the split-second capability to override impulses for more favorable options

fires—launches

focus/execute—the pattern of zeroing in and performing an action focus/execute, clear/repeat—the pattern of zeroing in, performing an action, clearing your head, and readying once again

frequency—the number of waves passing through a certain point in a specific span of time (e.g., light, sound, or electrical)

genetic engineering—manipulation of the genetic material of an organism

genome—an organism's complete set of DNA

genomics—the study of genes and how they work

gist—recognition meaning quickly or in a glance

glance—to look at something very quickly

glance information—detail gathered from a quick look

Golden Rule—the code of treating others as you want to be treated yourself

Hippocratic Oath—oath taken by doctors stating the proper conduct of their practice

homonyms—words with the same pronunciation yet different meanings—e.g., too, two, to

Human Genome Project—an international project to map the human genome

inattentional blindness—a phenomenon where one doesn't see new and unexpected things that suddenly appear in their field of vision, focusing on one thing that may cause you to lose focus on another

Inferno—Dante's story telling of a journey through Hell

informed-power—another name for energy which is composed of force directed by information

inhibition—blocking

internal chatter—self-talk

long-term memory—lasting memory storage

mindfulness—the energy (currency) of your presence

mirror neurons—circuit of brain cells on both sides of the brain

miser brain—see cognitive miser

monkey see, monkey do neurons—refers to mirror neurons

monochord—ancient acoustic, single-string musical instrument

motherese—simple, soothing sounds mothers (and fathers) make to infants

mushin—Japanese for empty mind, pure awareness without thought

negative priming—ignoring or blocking a certain detail resulting in the brain inhibiting that detail later

neurotransmitters—chemical messengers in the nervous system

optimism bias—type of bias that, in general, has us thinking we are less likely to experience a negative event or outcome to what we do

oxytocin—hormone secreted by the pituitary gland

pathology—pattern or patterns

perception—perceiving or interpreting information

positive psychology—the study of strengths of behavior and character that help individuals perform optimally and strive

premortem—a type of managerial visualization to help you determine what might cause a certain upcoming decision to fail so that you better navigate through it as it develops

psychological currency—mental and emotional energy

reflection—visualizing or thinking over specifics of a scenario after the fact resonance—a core element of music, the duration or reverberation of a note

rhythm—a core element of music, a pattern or repeating beat

salient—detail that stands out, is noticeable

selective attention—the ability to choose what information we want to attend to

self-scan—an attention training activity to help inventory what's going on in your head

serotonin—a hormone sometimes called the happy hormone because of its contributions to sleep and good moods

social referencing—analyzing cues from people in your environment

spatial relations—the position and relationship of objects in a given space

squashing—a process to compact information

squashing mechanism—a mental mechanism to filter information

synchrony—a core element of music, refers to coordination of all elements of the piece

Taoism—Chinese philosophy based on the Tao Te Ching

template—pattern for behavior

testosterone—sex hormone mostly associated with men

theta—theta waves, brain waves that are associated with the deep, relaxed state of mind in which you feel somewhere between wakefulness and sleep; sometimes referred to as dreamer's brain

tight lens—narrowed, concentrated attention

top-down biasing—cues to guide your attention to emerging detail

top-down processing—information processing based on previous knowledge, experience, expectations, and plans ultimatum game—commonly used economics game

visual pop-outs—when one visual target stands out over other dif-
fering ones

visualization—the process of using mental imagery or other sensory information to see yourself, another individual, or a situation
and so forth within a specific experience

waggle dance—dance performed by bees, can communicate the
direction toward a nectar-rich flower patch

whale songs—pattern of sounds (we call them songs) made by
whales to communicate

wide & narrow focus training—the practice of broadening or concentrating your attentional spotlight

wide lens—a broad attentional spotlight

working memory—short-term memory storage, short-term depot
for information, for example, while carrying out a task

zombie agents—term coined by Francis Crick and Christof Koch
to refer to routine behaviors that we perform constantly without
any thought; we just do it without awareness

ABOUT THE AUTHOR

Joseph Cardillo, PhD, is a top-selling author in the fields of health, mind-body-spirit, and psychology. An expert in Attention Training™, Joseph has taught his methods to more than twenty thousand students at various colleges, universities and institutions. His books have been translated into ten languages. His most notable work is the body-energy classic *Be Like Water (2003)*. His most recent book *Body Intelligence—Harness Your Body's Energies for Your Best Life (2015)* received a starred review in *Publishers Weekly*. He appears in football hall of famer Michael Strahan's book *Wake Up Happy* (2015) as an energy management expert and is a regular contributor to *Psychology Today*. He holds a PhD in holistic psychology and mind-body medicine.

**Visit JosephCardillo.com
to learn more about his work.**

ACKNOWLEDGMENTS

I wish to thank my immediate family for their energies, guidance and support in bringing this project to completion. Special thanks are extended to my wife, Elaine, for her brilliance and love along this journey; and to our beautiful and spirited daughters, Isabella and Veronica for all their goodness, magnificence and peace. We all had many conversations about human and non-human attention, some of it academic…but some also just for fun, some funny and some as we enjoyed it playing out in the world we traversed together. I thank my family for their patience in my quest and for jumping in and enjoying parts of it with me.

Thanks to all my martial arts, tai chi, and chi kung associates, partners, and colleagues for their support, brotherhood and sisterhood.

Special thanks to my agent, Linda Konner, for her great insights and vision toward this book and for her positivity, love of life, and encouragement throughout this project.

Special thanks to Iain Campbell, Publishing Director, for his vision and support—without which this project would not have been possible—and for his belief in placing its ideas into public dialogue especially during this time and place in history; Michelle Surianello, Senior US Production and Operations Manager, for keeping the entire project organized and flowing from beginning to end, for adding clarity whenever necessary over our many phone calls and emails and for her ongoing creativity and congeniality; and Sarah Burke, Marketing Associate, whose sparkling energy, resilient positivity and creativity was indispensible to this project.

I want to extend thanks to the editorial staff, Emily Frisella—editorial assistant, Jeanne Gibson- proofreader, and Renee Nicholls- copyeditor, all of whom worked long hours taking care to help guide and sharpen the ideas within this book, which could get complex at times, so that they came out clearly as possible; to Melissa Carl, sales manager, for her strategic and creative thinking to help get the book out to the public; to Aaron Munday, cover designer, for designing such a vibrant and fun cover; Jouve for typesetting the text into a format we can all enjoy; and to all at Nicholas Brealey and Hachette Books for sharing this vision; and to the energy that touched me in conversations quite a while ago with my wife and daughters that generated the first sparks for writing this book.

It is with deep gratitude that I acknowledge my parents, Alfio and Josephine Cardillo for their gifts of love and encouragement and life.

NOTES

Introduction

1. Jen Hubley Luckwaldt, "Learn This One Skill and Be More Successful at Work," PayScale, October 26, 2017, https://www.pay scale.com/career-news/2017/10/learn-one-skill-successful-work.
2. Ibid.
3. Molly Pennington, PhD, "25 of the Hardest Riddles Ever. Can You Solve Them?" *Reader's Digest,* accessed January 7, 2020, https://www.rd.com/funny-stuff/challenging-riddles/19/.
4. Julie Ray, "Americans' Stress, Worry and Anger Intensified in 2018," Gallup, April 25, 2019, https://news.gallup.com/poll/249098 /americans-stress-worry-anger-intensified-2018.aspx.
5. Jack Kelly, "More than Half of U.S. Workers Are Unhappy in Their Jobs: Here's Why and What Needs to Be Done Now," *Forbes,* October 25, 2019, https://www.forbes.com/sites/jackkelly/2019 /10/25/more-than-half-of-us-workers-are-unhappy-in-their-jobs -heres-why-and-what-needs-to-be-done-now/#787051d82024.
6. Joseph Cardillo, "Creativity: I Felt I Was Living a Double Life," *Psychology Today,* April 29, 2018, https://www.psychologytoday .com/intl/blog/attention-training/201804/creativity-i-felt-i -was-living-double-life?amp.

Chapter One

1. Steve Taylor, PhD, "Benjamin Libet and the Denial of Free Will," *Psychology Today,* September 5, 2017, https://www.psychologytoday .com/us/blog/out-the-darkness/201709/benjamin-libet-and-the -denial-free-will.
2. Ibid.

Chapter Two

1. Naotsugu Tsuchiya and Dr. Christof Koch, "Attention and Consciousness," Scholarpedia, May 5, 2008, http://www.scholarpedia.org/article/Attention_and_consciousness.

2. Ibid.

3. Joseph Cardillo, *Be Like Water* (New York: Grand Central, 2003), page 4.

4. Alessandra Zarcone, Marten van Schijndel, Jorrig Vogels, and Vera Demberg, "Salience and Attention in Surprisal-Based Accounts of Language Processing," *Frontiers in Psychology,* June 6, 2016, https://www.frontiersin.org/articles/10.3389/fpsyg.2016.00844/full.

5. Caroline Radnofsky and Caitlin Fichtel, "Flight Attendant Spills Drinks on American Airlines CEO," NBC News, April 10, 2019, https://www.nbcnews.com/news/us-news/flight-attendant-spills-drinks-american-airlines-ceo-n992876.

6. Peter Martinez, "Flight Attendant Spills Drinks on Her Airline's CEO: 'I WAS MORTIFIED,'" CBS News, April 10, 2019, https://www.cbsnews.com/news/flight-attendant-spills-drink-american-airlines-ceo-doug-parker-instagram-maddie-peters/.

7. Radnofsky and Fichtel, "Flight Attendant Spills Drinks."

8. Michael Graziano, "Your Brain Sees Things that You Don't," *Atlantic,* April 6, 2016, https://www.theatlantic.com/science/archive/2016/04/awareness-and-attention/476943/.

9. Ibid.

10. Ibid.

11. Association for Psychological Science, "Attention and Awareness Aren't the Same," June 6, 2011, https://www.psychologicalscience.org/news/releases/attention-and-awareness-arent-the-same.html.

12. David Biello, "Subliminal Nude Pictures Focus Attention," *Scientific American*, October 23, 2006, https://www.scientificamerican.com/article/subliminal-nude-pictures/.

13. Ibid.

14. Ibid.

15. Association for Psychological Science, "Your Brain Can Pay Attention to Something Without You Being Aware that It's There," Science Daily, June 6, 2011, https://www.sciencedaily.com/releases/2011/06/110606122253.htm.

16. Ibid.

17. Victor Lipman, "All Successful Leaders Need This Quality: Self-Awareness," *Forbes*, November 18, 2013, Leadership Strategy, https://www.forbes.com/sites/victorlipman/2013/11/18/all-successful-leaders-need-this-quality-self-awareness/#38ddecea1f06.

18. Julie Gordon, "Self-awareness in the Workplace," People Development Network, January 31, 2020, https://peopledevelopment magazine.com/2019/05/25/self-awareness-workplace/.

19. Ibid; Tasha Eurich, "What Self-Awareness Really Is (and How to Cultivate It)," *Harvard Business Review*, January 4, 2018, https://hbr.org/2018/01/what-self-awareness-really-is-and-how-to-cultivate-it.

20. Ibid.

Chapter Three

1. Christof Koch, *Consciousness: Confessions of a Romantic Reductionist* (Cambridge, MA: MIT Press, 2012), 78.

2. Bill Hutchinson, via GMA, "'All the Pieces Had to Come Together': Capt. Chesley 'Sully' Sullenberger Says on 10th Anniversary of Miraculous Hudson River Landing," ABC News, January 15, 2019, https://abcnews.go.com/GMA/News/pieces-capt-chesley-sully-sullenberger-10th-anniversary-miraculous/story?id=60334892.

3. Ibid.

4. Ibid.

5. Ibid.

6. John A. Bargh and Tanya Chartrand, "The Unbearable Automaticity of Being," *American Psychologist* 54, no. 7 (July 1999): 463, accessed February 1, 2020, https://acmelab.yale.edu/sites/default/files/1999_the_unbearable_automaticity_of_being.pdf.

Chapter Four

1. Olga Khazan, "Why Mistakes Are Often Repeated," *Atlantic*, February 25, 2016, accessed February 2, 2020, https://www.theatlantic.com/science/archive/2016/02/why-mistakes-are-often-repeated/470778/.

2. Ibid.

3. "Concentration," International Tennis Foundation, November 2019, https://www.itftennis.com/media/2165/psychology-concentration .pdf.

4. "All Songs +1: A Conversation with Paul McCartney," *All Songs Considered,* NPR (National Public Radio), June 10, 2016, https://www.npr.org/sections/allsongs/2016/06/10/481256944/all -songs-1-a-conversation-with-paul-mccartney.

5. "Paul McCartney Breaks Down His Most Iconic Songs," YouTube, September 11, 2018, video, https://www.youtube.com/watch ?v=u97_inloBmY.

6. Alison Doyle, "Workplace Flexibility Definition, Skills, and Examples," The Balance Careers, updated October 21, 2019, https://www.thebalancecareers.com/workplace-flexibility -definition-with-examples-2059699.

7. Ibid.

8. Kevin Loria, "These 18 Accidental and Unintended Scientific Discoveries Changed the World," *Business Insider,* April 4, 2018, https://www.businessinsider.com.au/viagra-lsd-pacemakers -accidental-scientific-discoveries-2018-4?r=US&IR=T.

9. "About *Christmas in the Air,*" Hallmark, accessed July 30, 2019, https://www.hallmarkmoviesandmysteries.com/christmas-in -the-air/about-christmas-in-the-air.

Chapter Five

1. DNA Learning Center, "Concept 18: Bacteria and Viruses Have DNA Too," Cold Spring Harbor Laboratory, accessed August 11, 2019, https://dnalc.cshl.edu/view/16394-Concept-18-Bacteria-and -viruses-have-DNA-too-.html.

2. Ibid.

3. "What Is a Genome?" NIH, US National Library of Medicine, accessed August 14, 2019, https://ghr.nlm.nih.gov/primer/hgp /genome.

4. "What Was the Human Genome Project and Why Has It Been Important?" NIH, US National Library of Medicine, accessed August 14, 2019, https://ghr.nlm.nih.gov/primer/hgp /description.

5. Aída Falcón de Vargas, "The Human Genome Project and Its Importance in Clinical Medicine," *Science Direct*, Elsevier, International Congress Series, Volume 1237, July 2002, pages 3–13, https://www.sciencedirect.com/science/article/abs/pii/S0531513101005702.

6. Vivek Nityananda, "Attention-Like Processes in Insects," *Proceedings Biological Sciences* 283, National Center for Biotechnology Information (NCBI), November 16, 2016, https://www.ncbi.nlm.nih.gov/pmc/articles/PMC5124100/.

7. Kara McGrath, Bustle, "The Origin of 'Float Like a Butterfly, Sting Like a Bee' Proved Muhammad Ali's Greatness Early On," Bustle, June 4, 2016, https://www.bustle.com/articles/164846-the-origin-of-float-like-a-butterfly-sting-like-a-bee-proved-muhammad-alis-greatness-early.

8. Harry Haroutioun Haladjian, PhD, "Consciousness in Other Animals," *Psychology Today,* April 3, 2017. https://www.psychologytoday.com/us/blog/theory-consciousness/201704/consciousness-in-other-animals.

9. Nityananda, "Attention-Like Processes in Insects."

10. Ibid.

11. Andrew B. Barron, "Insects Have the Capacity for Subjective Experience." Full article: file:///C:/Users/CIGYA/Downloads/KleinBarrononInsectExperience-3%20(1).pdf. Page4. Accessed March 5, 2020. Originally accessed from Research Gate, https://www.researchgate.net/figure/The-vertebrate-behavioral-core-control-system-Following-Merker-2007-autonomous-animal_fig1_311770445, March 5, 2020.

12. Christof Koch (interviewed by Steve Paulson), "How Do We Wrap Our Minds Around Bee Consciousness?" *To the Best of Our Knowledge,* May 17, 2019, https://www.ttbook.org/interview/how-do-we-wrap-our-minds-around-bee consciousness.

13. Lars Chittka, "Bee Cognition," *Current Biology* 27 (October 9, 2017), accessed February 2, 2020, https://www.cell.com/current-biology/pdf/S0960-9822(17)31017-5.pdf.

14. Elizabeth G. Dunn, "What Lonely Humans Can Learn From Lonely Mice," *Elemental,* December 5, 2018, https://elemental.medium.com/what-lonely-humans-can-learn-from-lonely-mice-1c412f5b1d81.

15. Ibid.

16. Brian M. Sweis, Mark J. Thomas, and A. David Redish, "Mice Learn to Avoid Regret," *PLoS Biology* 16 (6), June 21, 2018, https://journals.plos.org/plosbiology/article?id=10.1371/journal.pbio.2005853.

17. Louis D. Matzel et al., "Longitudinal Attentional Engagement Rescues Mice from Age-related Cognitive Declines and Cognitive Inflexibility," *Learning Memory* 18, no. 5 (May 2011): 345–356, https://www.ncbi.nlm.nih.gov/pmc/articles/PMC3083642/.

18. Tara Parker-Pope. "Vigorous Exercise Linked with Better Grades." *New York Times.* June 3, 2010, Well, https://well.blogs.nytimes.com/2010/06/03/vigorous-exercise-linked-with-better-grades/. Accessed March 10, 2020.

19. Ashleigh Johnstone. "Martial Arts Offers Brain-Boosting Benefits for All Ages, Research Finds." May 14, 2018. *The Independent.* https://www.independent.co.uk/life-style/health-and-families/healthy-living/martial-arts-physical-mental-benefits-health-exercise-tai-chi-karate-a8342756.html. Accessed March 11, 2020.

20. E. Paul Zehr, PhD. "Martial Arts Training Can Help Autism." *Psychology Today.* October 29, 2016. https://www.psychologytoday.com/us/blog/black-belt-brain/201610/martial-arts-training-can-help-autism. Accessed March 11, 2020.

21. "Dancing and the Brain." Harvard Mahoney Neuroscience Institute, *On the Brain* newsletter. https://neuro.hms.harvard.edu/harvard-mahoney-neuroscience-institute/brain-newsletter/and-brain/dancing-and-brain. Accessed March 11, 2020.

22. Coren Stanley, PhD, DSc, "How Does a Dog's Attention Vary over Its Lifetime?" *Psychology Today,* April 7, 2014, https://www.psychologytoday.com/us/blog/canine-corner/201404/how-does-dogs-attention-vary-over-its-lifetime.

23. Coren Stanley, PhD, DSc, "Your Dog Watches You and Interprets Your Behavior," *Psychology Today,* April 7, 2014, https://www.psychologytoday.com/us/blog/canine-corner/201210/your-dog-watches-you-and-interprets-your-behavior.

24. Nicola Davis, "Dogs Have Pet Facial Expressions to Use on Humans, Study Finds," *The Guardian,* October 19, 2017,

https://www.theguardian.com/science/2017/oct/19/dogs-have-pet-facial-expressions-to-use-on-humans-study-finds.

25. Ibid.

26. Katito N. Sayialel, and Cynthia Moss, "Elephants Can Determine Ethnicity, Gender, and Age from Acoustic Cues in Human Voices," PNAS, April 8, 2014 111 (14) 5433-5438, https://www.pnas.org/content/111/14/5433.

27. "Greek Medicine," translated by Michael North, US National Library of Medicine, updated February 7, 2012, https://www.nlm.nih.gov/hmd/greek/greek_oath.html.

Chapter Six

1. Sony Pictures. *Run Lola Run*, https://www.sonypictures.com/movies/runlolarun, Accessed March 10, 2020.

2. Kansas State University, Visual Cognition Laboratory, "Recognizing the Gist of a Scene," accessed September 3, 2019, https://www.k-state.edu/psych/vcl/basic-research/scene-gist.html.

3. Li Fei-Fei, Asha Iyer, Christof Koch, and Pietro Perona, "What Do We Perceive in a Glance of a Real-World Scene?" *Journal of Vision* 7, no. 1 (January 2007), https://jov.arvojournals.org/article.aspx?articleid=2192891#133661152.

4. Wayne Drehs, "Ryan Lochte, Michael Phelps Separated by Fraction of a Second," ESPN Sports, July 1, 2016, https://www.espn.com/olympics/swimming/story/_/id/16684730/2016-us-olympic-swim-trials-ryan-lochte-cherishes-racing-michael-phelps.

5. Ibid.

6. Nicholas O. Rule, Michael L. Slepian, and Nalini Ambady, "A Memory Advantage for Untrustworthy Faces," *Cognition* 125, no. 2 (November 2012): 207–218, https://www.sciencedirect.com/science/article/abs/pii/S0010027712001400?via%3Dihub.

7. Ibid.

8. Katherine Dill, "Never Give a Boring Presentation Again," Forbes, April 27, 2016, https://www.forbes.com/sites/kathryndill/2016/04/27/never-give-a-boring-presentation-again-3/#3cb8d4656e24.

Chapter Seven

1. "Best News Bloopers June 2019 Will Make Your Summer," YouTube, July 3, 2019, video, https://www.youtube.com/watch?v=4xqEd3ElWJA.
2. Ibid.
3. Julie Ray, "Americans' Stress, Worry and Anger Intensified in 2018," Gallup, April 25, 2019, https://news.gallup.com/poll/249098/americans-stress-worry-anger-intensified-2018.aspx.

Chapter Eight

1. Peter Johansson and Lars Hall, "The Choice Blindness Lab," LUCS: Lund University Cognitive Science, January 7, 2020, https://www.lucs.lu.se/choice-blindness-group/.
2. Ibid.
3. "Bet You Didn't Notice 'The Invisible Gorilla,'" *Talk of the Nation,* NPR (National Public Radio), May 19, 2010, https://www.npr.org/templates/story/story.php?storyId=126977945.
4. Jack B. Soll, Katherine L. Milkman, and John W. Payne, "Outsmart Your Own Biases," *Harvard Business Review,* May 2015, https://hbr.org/2015/05/outsmart-your-own-biases.
5. Ibid.
6. Christy Nicholson, "Memory and Consciousness: Consciousness to Unconsciousness and Back Again," Association for Psychological Science, August 2006, https://www.psychologicalscience.org/observer/memory-and-consciousness-consciousness-to-unconsciousness-and-back-again.
7. Ibid.
8. Joseph Cardillo, *Can I Have Your Attention? How to Think Fast, Find Your Focus, and Sharpen Your Concentration* (Newburyport, MA: Redwheel/Weiser, 2009), 128–29.
9. Ibid, 130.
10. Brad Tuttle, "Warren Buffett's Boring, Brilliant Wisdom," *Time,* March 1, 2010, https://business.time.com/2010/03/01/warren-buffetts-boring-brilliant-wisdom/.

Chapter Nine

1. Cardillo, Joseph, *Can I Have Your Attention? How to Think Fast, Find Your Focus, and Sharpen Your Concentration* (Newburyport, MA: Redwheel/Weiser, 2009).
2. Christina Fink, PhD; Emily Galvin, MS; and Temple Wise, "Shifting Between Broad and Narrow Focus," YSC Sports Mental Edge (blog), WordPress.com, June 9, 2015, https://yscsportsmentaledge.wordpress.com/2015/06/09/shifting-between-broad-and-narrow-focus/.
3. Daniel Goleman, *Focus: The Hidden Driver of Excellence* (New York: HarperCollins, 2015), 27.
4. Ibid.
5. Laurent Itti and Ali Borji. "Computational Models: Bottom-Up and Top-Down Aspects," PDF, University of Southern California, accessed March 4, 2020, http://ilab.usc.edu/borji/papers/paper.pdf.
6. Ibid.
7. Thomas Hout and David Michael, "A Chinese Approach to Management," *Harvard Business Review,* September 2014, accessed March 5, 2020, https://hbr.org/2014/09/a-chinese-approach-to-management.

Chapter Ten

1. Joseph Cardillo, *Can I Have Your Attention? How to Think Fast, Find Your Focus, and Sharpen Your Concentration* (Newburyport, MA: Redwheel/Weiser, 2009), 105.
2. Daniel Goleman, *Emotional Intelligence: Why It Can Matter More than IQ* (New York: Bantam, 2005), 45.
3. Tamar Chansky, PhD, "Rethinking the Path to Empathy," *Psychology Today,* July 8, 2019, https://www.psychologytoday.com/us/blog/worry-wise/201907/rethinking-the-path-empathy.
4. Donald Pfaff, *The Neuroscience of Fair Play: Why We (Usually) Follow the Golden Rule* (New York: Dana Press, 2007).
5. Ibid.

6. David Freedberg and Vittorio Gallese, "Motion, Emotion and Empathy in Aesthetic Experience," *Trends in Cognitive Sciences* 11, (May 2007): 197–203, https://www.researchgate.net/publication /263809628_Motion_Emotion_and_Empathy_in_Aesthetic _Experience_D_Freedberg_and_V_Gallese.

7. Ibid., quote by L. B. Alberti.

Chapter Eleven

1. Buster Benson, "You Are Almost Definitely Not Living in Reality Because Your Brain Doesn't Want You To," Quartz, September 16, 2016, https://qz.com/776168/a-comprehensive-guide-to -cognitive-biases/.

2. Darcy Jacobsen, "8 Cognitive Biases that Will Make or Break Your Culture," Workhuman, September 11, 2012, https://www .workhuman.com/resources/globoforce-blog/8-cognitive-biases -that-will-make-or-break-your-culture.

3. William M. P. Klein and Peter R. Harris. "Self-Affirmation Enhances Attentional Bias Toward Threatening Components of a Persuasive Message," *Psychological Science* 20, no. 12 (December 1, 2009). https://journals.sagepub.com/doi/10.1111/j.1467-9280.2009 .02467.x

4. Ibid.

5. Laura Kress and Tatjana Aue, "The Link Between Optimism Bias and Attention Bias: A Neurocognitive Perspective," *Neuroscience and Biobehavioral Reviews* 80, (September 2017): 688–702, https://www.sciencedirect.com/science/article/pii/S014976341 6306406?via%3Dihub.

6. Ibid.

7. Ibid.

8. Tali Sharot, "The Optimism Bias," TED2012, video, 17:34, February 2012, https://www.ted.com/talks/tali_sharot_the_optimism _bias?language=en.

9. Ibid.

INDEX